FROM

MOM LIFE

MY JOURNEY THROUGH
PREGNANCY, NATURAL
CHILDBIRTH, AND MY BABY'S
FIRST MILESTONES

BARBIE FAMIGLIETTI

FROM MY LIFE TO MOM LIFE
Copyright © 2021 by Barbie Famiglietti

Library of Congress Control Number: 2021905708
ISBN: 978-0-578-86564-5

First Edition: April 2021

Edited by Dr. Carrie McDermott Goldman
Photos by Peter Famiglietti and Jenifer Landis
Cover design by www.chainzown.com

1 2 3 4 5 6 7 8 9 10

For My Little Family

TABLE OF CONTENTS

GETTING PREGNANT

1   SOMETIMES THERE IS HARDSHIP BEFORE BLESSINGS
7   IF A FAMILY IS WHAT YOU WANT, DON'T EVER STOP TRYING
18   PRESSING ON THIS UPHILL BATTLE

NINE MONTH BABY BUILDING

29   EAT WELL, BE WELL
36   MOISTURIZE LIKE NO TOMORROW!
41   LET THE NESTING BEGIN
65   GRAB ALL THE KNOWLEDGE YOU CAN, WHERE YOU CAN
74   A BIRTH PLAN: WHAT IS IT, AND WHY YOU NEED ONE
91   PREPARATION WAS THE KEY FOR ME

MY NATURAL BIRTH

104   IT'S SHOWTIME!
115   MY BREASTFEEDING TIPS THAT WORKED
123   TAKING MY BABY HOME
132   WHAT I WISH I KNEW BEFORE I WAS IN IT

MY NEW MOM LIFE

142   GETTING MY BABY TO SLEEP, AND SLEEP WELL
151   HUNGRY MOMMA FOOD PREP
161   IN THE BEGINNING, DELIVER EVERYTHING
169   MAKING MY OWN BABY FOOD
188   THE END OF AN ERA
197   NEW ADVENTURES WITH MY BABY
205   GETTING YOURSELF TOGETHER

215   ACKNOWLEDGEMENTS
219   RESOURCES
220   CONNECT ON SOCIAL MEDIA

In this book, you will learn how to stay calm, get prepared, and how to set up your house to receive a new baby, without disrupting the beautiful balance of your marriage. Childbirth is not a dramatic, horrific, scream at the top of your lungs, event that will leave you sobbing in a ball in the corner. Although, Hollywood has programmed us to believe it IS the scariest, hardest thing you will ever do in your life, as a woman. (And special effects make it the grossest, bloodiest thing you will ever witness.) I am here to tell you that is false. It is possible to have a calm and peaceful birth. Certainly there are some women who have very traumatic birthing experiences for a variety of reasons: emergencies, unforeseen circumstances, etc. But that is not what this book is about. I want to let you know there is another way. A peaceful and calm way. I did not come out of the delivery room crumbled, broken and distraught wondering "What the hell just happened?"

No one tells you the beauty, the strength, or the resilience childbirth brings to your heart. Holding that baby for the first time and seeing this child that rode around inside you for nine months makes you feel proud. You carried this baby. You spoke to this baby.

You loved your baby before you even met. It is, in a word, **AMAZING.**

TRIGGER WARNING

The first few chapters talk about my struggles getting pregnant and staying pregnant. I walk you through my two miscarriages and explain how I successfully carried my third pregnancy to term. I share these hardships because it is part of my baby journey. But I understand completely if you do not wish to read about this sadness. If you are a first time mom-to-be and you picked up this book to learn how to prepare for your baby, you are still in the right book. Just skip to Chapter 3, I won't be offended.

1

SOMETIMES THERE IS HARDSHIP BEFORE BLESSINGS

LET ME START AT THE VERY BEGINNING, well before I was pregnant with my baby. As emotionally painful as it feels to write about this, I still need to say it for the sake of others reading who may have struggled with the same thing. It is not taboo; it happens more than most people realize.

I married the love of my life, and within three months after our wedding, I got pregnant. We told our family and a few close friends. It was all very exciting! We went in for our first check-up at the OBGYN and I was eight weeks pregnant. We saw the fetus on the ultrasound, it looked like a little jelly bean, but there was no flashing light of a heartbeat and no sound. The doctor could not find the baby's heartbeat anywhere. We were devastated. They did some additional tests and even sent me to another specialist for a more detailed ultrasound to double and triple check the findings. All in the same day. As we waited in each waiting room, we just hugged each other, sobbing, not knowing this was even a possibility. It did not run in my family and never crossed my mind, not even once before this. When I got pregnant, I imagined staying pregnant until the baby was born.

After all the bloodwork, poking and prodding concluded, the answer was final: this was not a viable pregnancy and it would end in a miscarriage. Somehow, the fetus would have to exit my body. I had a few options: I could have a natural miscarriage at home, take a pill to force the miscarriage to come out within the next 24-48 hours, or get a D&C* procedure done where a doctor removes it for me.

INTRODUCTION

Every pregnant woman feels unprepared. I know I did. You may be thinking the same thing, going back and forth between excitement of what is to come, followed by fear of the unknown. Believe me, I was there too. Even though I had been trying to get pregnant for many years, and always knew I *wanted* to be a mother, in my mind I wondered if I was even cut out for this. Let me be the first to tell you, YES, you are cut out for this. We are women with a built-in mechanism called, "Mother's Instinct." I have heard of it, but saw it truly come to life when I had a child. It is a real thing and you need to trust it. Your instincts know what to do to care for your child. When your child is hungry, you will know what to do. When your baby is sick, you will know how to soothe them. Motherhood is beautiful and rewarding. Take peace in the fact that all the knowledge is within you. I am just here to put it all on paper for you.

I am a stay-at-home Mom who has, through plenty of trial and error, learned what works best for me on my motherhood journey. I believe researching information is my super power. I like to stay up late reading articles, googling solutions, and finding out how to overcome anything I may need help with. And when I find the answer, I can hardly wait to share it with my Mom Friends.

As a college grad from UCSB, I hold my degree in Environmental Science. Right after college I dove into the exercise and nutrition world. I worked as a Personal Trainer for many years and then became a Nutritionist at a university in New York. I have my Food Safety Certification and my husband has taught me many techniques in the kitchen, from his training in culinary school. We love to cook side by side, creating new healthy recipes together to feed our family. My career path meandered through many other jobs that included high-level customer service, property management, and even Real Estate. "Retiring" from it all to become a full-time mom has allowed me to pool all my skills together for my son.

So here is my new job description: I am a chef, a personal shopper, an educator, a professional laundry folder, housekeeper, bill payer, meal planner, scheduler (aka master of the family calendar), anger management specialist (for toddlers), organizer, bug collector, problem solver, bubble machine operator, and Crayola craft manager. All of my career paths I have ever been on, now boil down to one big title: MOM. The most important title I will ever have! I guess you could say I got a promotion, because I am now the CEO of my household.

Our son is three, as I write this, so you would think three years of experience might be a long time to figure things out. Sure, I feel more at peace about being a mom than I did the day I brought him home. But I am still learning every day and I don't think anyone ever has motherhood completely figured out. We are all here to teach each other. But, yes, I feel a little more confident in what I am doing than the day I gave birth. It certainly is a progression, kind of a learn-as-you-go walk through life. But the first four months after he was born were the hardest for me: trying to navigate through breastfeeding, sleep deprivation, and taking care of a tiny little dude. But once he started sleeping through the night at four months, and eating solid foods at six months, I could get back to a bit of normalcy in my life. Sure, I stumbled along the way, but reading articles, books, speaking to other moms who have gone before me, and the internet, allowed me to pull it all together. My mom and sister were very instrumental for me since they both had three kids each. So yeah, I had two pros in my corner which helped me so much.

Since I did the research already, I have put it all together for you in one book. My goal is to share every bit of knowledge, every morsel I learned with YOU. Every piece of equipment I used personally, that I could not live without. Motherhood can be smooth, calm, and collected if you prepare for it. These are all the things I wish I knew before having a baby. It is my hope by you reading my book, you will feel less overwhelmed, and more confident about giving birth. I share because this is the book I WISH I had before giving birth.

In this book, you will learn how to stay calm, get prepared, and how to set up your house to receive a new baby, without disrupting the beautiful balance of your marriage. Childbirth is not a dramatic, horrific, scream at the top of your lungs, event that will leave you sobbing in a ball in the corner. Although, Hollywood has programmed us to believe it IS the scariest, hardest thing you will ever do in your life, as a woman. (And special effects make it the grossest, bloodiest thing you will ever witness.) I am here to tell you that is false. It is possible to have a calm and peaceful birth. Certainly there are some women who have very traumatic birthing experiences for a variety of reasons: emergencies, unforeseen circumstances, etc. But that is not what this book is about. I want to let you know there is another way. A peaceful and calm way. I did not come out of the delivery room crumbled, broken and distraught wondering "What the hell just happened?"

No one tells you the beauty, the strength, or the resilience childbirth brings to your heart. Holding that baby for the first time and seeing this child that rode around inside you for nine months makes you feel proud. You carried this baby. You spoke to this baby.

You loved your baby before you even met. It is, in a word, **AMAZING.**

TRIGGER WARNING

The first few chapters talk about my struggles getting pregnant and staying pregnant. I walk you through my two miscarriages and explain how I successfully carried my third pregnancy to term. I share these hardships because it is part of my baby journey. But I understand completely if you do not wish to read about this sadness. If you are a first time mom-to-be and you picked up this book to learn how to prepare for your baby, you are still in the right book. Just skip to Chapter 3, I won't be offended.

1

SOMETIMES THERE IS HARDSHIP BEFORE BLESSINGS

LET ME START AT THE VERY BEGINNING, well before I was pregnant with my baby. As emotionally painful as it feels to write about this, I still need to say it for the sake of others reading who may have struggled with the same thing. It is not taboo; it happens more than most people realize.

I married the love of my life, and within three months after our wedding, I got pregnant. We told our family and a few close friends. It was all very exciting! We went in for our first check-up at the OBGYN and I was eight weeks pregnant. We saw the fetus on the ultrasound, it looked like a little jelly bean, but there was no flashing light of a heartbeat and no sound. The doctor could not find the baby's heartbeat anywhere. We were devastated. They did some additional tests and even sent me to another specialist for a more detailed ultrasound to double and triple check the findings. All in the same day. As we waited in each waiting room, we just hugged each other, sobbing, not knowing this was even a possibility. It did not run in my family and never crossed my mind, not even once before this. When I got pregnant, I imagined staying pregnant until the baby was born.

After all the bloodwork, poking and prodding concluded, the answer was final: this was not a viable pregnancy and it would end in a miscarriage. Somehow, the fetus would have to exit my body. I had a few options: I could have a natural miscarriage at home, take a pill to force the miscarriage to come out within the next 24-48 hours, or get a D&C* procedure done where a doctor removes it for me.

*According to **www.mayoclinic.org** the definition of D&C is the following:

*"Dilation and curettage (**D&C**) is a **procedure** to remove tissue from inside your uterus. Doctors perform dilation and curettage to diagnose and treat certain uterine conditions — such as heavy bleeding — or to clear the uterine lining after a miscarriage or abortion."*

These were all tough choices. I had no idea which one to choose quite yet. My thoughts were jumbled and I really could not seem to process this new information. I needed more support. I wanted a second professional opinion, and I was about to get one. My very next appointment I had planned that day, was to a doula, who delivered my sister's kids. (For those of you who do not know what a doula is, it's someone who delivers babies outside of the hospital. Usually in a birthing center or in your home. This doula had her own birthing center, close to our home. I wanted the most natural birth possible, so this would have been it.)

A few hours after this horrible news, I had to face the doula and explain to her, through my tears, what we just learned that morning. Unfortunately, this is where our relationship had to end. It is too much of a liability for her to work with someone who has a miscarriage. I got placed into a "high risk category" and there I would stay for the rest of my days. If I got pregnant again, I would have to automatically give birth in a hospital and the natural option I had hoped for was out the window. I understood her position, but it was just another piece of bad news I did not want to hear in that moment. After this appointment, I went with my gut. I wanted to go home, and have the miscarriage naturally with no pills, no help. Just let my body pass it in its own time. That is exactly what I did.

In hindsight, I would not choose passing the miscarriage at home. It happened about a week later. But it was very hard not knowing when it was going to happen, how it was going to feel, or where I was even going to be when it started happening. Turns out, I was with a client at work when the pain started so bad, like I got kicked in the stomach. I smiled as best as I could, finished up the paperwork, then shooed him out of my office and locked up. I was bent over on the office floor when I called my husband. He came right away. I hobbled to the bathroom and went right to the toilet. There was so much blood and it was so painful I just had to sit there and let it pass. It took about 20 minutes sitting on the toilet and multiple toilet flushes later, for the pain to finally subside, before I could make my way home.

It was so hard to walk and my husband helped me make it home. Thankfully, I worked in the office of the apartment complex where I lived, so it was a short walk home. But it was the longest walk of my life. When we got to the stairs, my dear husband carried me up to the third floor! I did not have the strength to walk up a single step. I stumbled to the bathroom and had more tissue to pass. It was four hours of toilet, bed, toilet, shower, toilet, bed, shower, over and over. I tried to take a few bites of food in between to get some strength and a few sips of water to rehydrate. The cramps were unbelievable! The amount of blood was like having a heavy period times 100! This was the most pain I had ever felt, in my entire life.

Once it was over, the following days, weeks and months were emotionally draining. My husband and I prayed a lot together, cried a lot together, and wondered what the future held for us. I saw so many doctors and specialists I lost count. Not a single doctor I met could tell me *why* I had a miscarriage. Everyone just kept saying, "Well, the good news is, you got pregnant. Just keep trying!" This was not comforting to me at all. And certainly, did not feel like good news. I wanted answers!

What helped me get my mind off things and move forward was throwing my sister a surprise baby shower for her second child. I tried very hard to find joy in other women's ability to have children, while I knew I could not. It was an internal struggle, but I knew I had to rise above and not let this get me down, and keep me down. Doing this for her helped me feel better. She enjoyed the shower and I really did have a lot of fun planning it. She had a beautiful baby girl one month later.

2

IF A FAMILY IS WHAT YOU WANT, DON'T EVER STOP TRYING

About five months later I became pregnant a second time. But the feeling was completely different. I did not enter the doctor's office with excitement, joy, and elation, to then get blindsided by no heartbeat. This time I was full of hesitation, fear, anxiety, and uncertainty. Inside I felt divided in half equally: fifty percent of me was hopeful with faith and peace, that this was the time we would bring a beautiful baby into the world. I would take this pregnancy all the way to term, for sure! The other fifty percent was sure this would be another loss, another dark place, another stake through my heart.

I was six weeks pregnant and I decided not to tell my family about it until after this appointment. Sitting in the waiting room was difficult because I just wanted to know already. My mind kept switching between this will be a good appointment and the pregnancy will be fine to prepare yourself for devastation, as this could be a repeat of last time. But it's in God's hands, whatever it is I am ready for it. No, I was SO not ready, I wanted to go home! No, I wanted to know, I had to stay there! Just power through, stay strong. But through all the back and forth emotions, I knew my man was here with me and we could get through anything together!

Finally, they called us, I changed into my hospital gown and geared up to have the vaginal ultrasound to check on the fetus. While we waited for the doctor to come into the room, my husband and I were either drumming our fingers, or tapping our feet. We wanted the doctor to hurry up already and tell us the news. But I also didn't want to hear any bad news. The doctor came in to do the exam and found that this was not a viable pregnancy. No heartbeat or growth measured to where it "should be." This fetus stopped growing and was at a standstill. It wasn't even shaped like a fetus, more like a blob. My husband thought it looked like a bean. My heart shattered again. I could not even look at the monitor on this one. I did not want to connect with this baby blob. I just wanted to stay detached and I did. I believed it was for the best.

When it came time to make my decision of which path I wanted to take, I opted for the D&C this time. I did not want to miscarry at home, as that was super emotional and difficult the last time. If you do a D&C it is an in and out, same day procedure. They make you sign all these scary forms that say this procedure could end in a hysterectomy if something goes wrong. Forms that basically say you could die on the operating table. I even had to give permission to do a blood transfusion if I lost too much blood during the process. However, they were required and I signed my life away. I had to. I had no choice if I wanted to move forward. But it irked me that the "system" makes you sign these things to free *them* of all responsibility. I get it, but it makes a difficult and emotional decision even more difficult. I was terrified.

I called my mom and sister to tell them I was scheduled for surgery. They had no idea I was even pregnant, so of course it came as a shock. These were very hard calls to make, but I was thankful they were there for me. It is always good to have family support and I have been lucky enough to have them my whole life.

A few days later, I went in for my procedure. When I went under the anesthesia, my husband was there. When I woke up from surgery, he was there. I'm so thankful for my husband, who is my ROCK through thick and thin. As long as he is by my side, I know we can get through anything together.

I lived! And there were no complications. Now, all I had to do was focus on moving past this, emotionally, and see what the next step was for our family. Would it be adoption, In-Vetro-Fertilization (IVF), or try again? Only time would tell after I healed from this major setback.

PEOPLE CROSS OUR PATHS AT EXACTLY THE RIGHT MOMENTS

It took me five months to heal emotionally from these two losses. My husband and I prayed often. We spoke of the experience often, checking in on one another. Part of the healing process was making sure the other person was doing okay. There were days when I was super emotional and I would turn to him for support. As husband and wife, when once is weak the other is strong. We were able to find our balance again.

I did yoga and took walks with my dog. I tried to find the peace in nature, a sunset, a flower, or a shady tree. Once we got to a place of acceptance, we both felt deep in our bones that our journey was not over. We wanted to be parents. We were ready to move on and put the past behind us. We both felt ready to try to get pregnant again. But only to move forward, cautiously. Funny how in the face of tragedy and complete devastation, someone crosses your path that brings you renewed faith and hope. This someone was Dr. Julie Taylor.

She was an old friend I went to high school with who recently posted on Facebook that she was opening her practice as a holistic doctor. One of her specialties: helping women with hormonal imbalances. I had read about hormone imbalances years ago. And what seemed to be serendipity, I kept coming across more and more articles about it in places like my newsfeed or researching the internet. It made my ears perk up and I wanted to learn more. Perhaps this was something that could work. Perhaps this was the answer to why I kept losing pregnancies. I felt hopeful, as if it was God's way of nudging me in the right direction. I wrote her an email to see if she could help me. Her answer was yes.

After many types of testing (saliva, bloodwork, and urine) she determined that my hormones were very imbalanced, both estrogen and progesterone. Turns out, my progesterone was so low, it barely showed up on the chart. If a woman is trying to get pregnant but her progesterone is too low, the pregnancy most likely will not make it very far. The key is to get progesterone levels high enough to reach 12 weeks. (Past the first trimester.) After 12 weeks, the uterus starts to make its own progesterone and can continue to carry the baby to term without supplementation. This made sense to me! Dr. Taylor was the very first person who gave me a clear, concrete, scientific reason why my body could not hold a pregnancy. Our prayers had been answered and this gave me great hope! She had a plan and we just had to put it into action.

She put me on a natural hormone therapy replacement protocol with no side effects. One was an estrogen cream I would rub on my thighs every morning. The other was a pill of progesterone which I took every morning and every night before bed. These were made from things found in nature, not synthetics, and did not harm my body in any way. Specifically, the progesterone was made from yams. The official term for these substances is called "bioidentical hormones." This means your body recognizes them as your own hormones so it does not disturb you at all. Any woman who has ever taken synthetic hormones knows there are a slew of side effects that goes along with them. I had never tried synthetic hormones, but I read enough bad things about them. I was not interested in making matters worse for myself. This is why I steered away from conventional medicine and toward a more natural approach. I was so intrigued and happy to take part in this new journey with her. She came into my life at the perfect time, since I was fed up with conventional doctors. This was my new path and I was taking it!

A month later, I started the hormone therapy and my levels improved. We just went about our lives and I felt pretty great. We didn't think too much about trying to have a baby. In fact, we didn't even think about it at all. We had a fun year of moving into a new condo, decorating it, and doing lots of travel. We went on countless hiking trips, spent time visiting with family and friends and frequently took our dog, Zorra, to the beach. I quit my job and made a career change. My life was moving forward and staying busy was my coping mechanism. It worked and served as a much needed escape from the past two tragedies we had just lived through. Things were looking up and life was good!

The only downside to seeing Dr. Taylor, was that our insurance did NOT cover any of our medical expenses, and we had to pay for *everything* out of pocket. It was expensive, but in the grand scheme of things, it was worth every penny. From it came my little boy! My advice to anyone having fertility issues, is to keep going strong and persevere. Be innovative and do not stay within the "conventional" medical system. All that my regular doctor told me to do was to keep trying and take a baby aspirin every day to help with blood flow. Huh? That made no sense to me. I already had low blood pressure, and if baby aspirin acts like a blood thinner, I did not agree with this advice. I dug a little deeper online, only to find an aspirin a day is usually prescribed to older patients who have had a heart attack in the past. It helps them avoid another one and the age group is 50 – 70 years old.* I knew I didn't fall into that category!

*https://www.health.harvard.edu/staying-healthy/a-major-change-for-daily-aspirin-therapy

Obviously, we kept on trying but I never took the baby aspirin. When I switched doctors, I focused on getting my hormones right (I never knew they were out of whack before this), eating well, and making sweet love to my husband. And it worked! On New Year's Eve we had a wonderful night and we conceived.

Dr. Taylor wanted to know the minute I got pregnant so she could change up the way she was administering the progesterone hormone. When I missed my period in January and took a home pregnancy test to confirm I was, indeed, pregnant, I gave her a call. She had her holistic pharmacist whip up these vaginal suppositories for me. It is kind of a weird concept, but I was willing to give it a try. They were white, and the shape of a teeny, tiny tampon. They were natural, made from yams, and needed refrigeration. My instructions were to insert one every night before bed. The theory on this was to flood my uterus with progesterone, since my body was not producing nearly enough of its own to hold a pregnancy. The fetus needed lots of it to grow, sustain, and multiply cells in a healthy environment. This made sense to me. The past two pregnancies did not "take" because my own progesterone was so low, it could not sustain itself. At this point, I would try anything, and since this was natural, I was more than ok with it.

The first night, I laid in bed and inserted the first progesterone suppository. It was easy and I didn't feel it after it was in. It was kind of like a tampon that you cannot feel. But it scared me to move, as I did not want it to fall out or slide away from the uterus. I tried my best to go to sleep in whatever position I was in. I felt like a mannequin, not moving, but hey, whatever it takes! Night after night, I did this. Day after day I worried. Is this going to take? Will this process work? Dr. Taylor said to keep this up all the way until twelve weeks pregnant. Once you complete the first trimester, your body produces its own progesterone and I would not need these inserts anymore.

This time, I let my immediate family in on the process. I even brought my mom to a couple of appointments with me since Dr. Taylor was a childhood friend of mine. But I did not make my baby announcement until after the first trimester. Given my history, I wanted to be sure. And that is the typical time frame for most people, I think.

3

PRESSING ON THIS UPHILL BATTLE

There were a few scares during those 12 weeks. At one point, I went in to get my Human Chorionic Gonadotropin (HCG) levels checked. HCG is a hormone produced once implantation occurs in the uterus. This is the hormone measured by your standard home pregnancy test when you pee on the stick. When you are pregnant, this hormone should be doubling every couple of days and my levels were dropping. I called Dr. Taylor for her advice. She informed me to just keep doing the vaginal inserts and get checked again the following week. That was a LONG week! With a lot of prayer and inspiration, my husband and I made it through. And thankfully, the levels rose on the next HCG test. I also had a little spotting at times, which freaked me out. But I later learned spotting was also totally normal for most pregnancies.

The first 12 weeks felt like walking through a jungle filled with obstacles: quick sand, animal traps, wasp nests, land mines, and any other item that could completely destroy your life. All the while, I was trying to walk to the summit, the end of those first 12 weeks of pregnancy, without stepping on one of them. That summit, I imagined, would be a clearing of the jungle, bringing me to a cliff that met the ocean. With a breathtaking view, the sun on my face, and the taste of salty ocean air. It would be a feeling of peace to know that I made it to the second trimester. Only then would it be time to feel all the joy and happiness a pregnant mother is supposed to feel. I did not want to allow myself to feel this until I knew I was in the clear. Not yet, it was too soon.

It was an emotional roller coaster since I wanted so badly to be happy and joyful. But I was afraid to get too attached to this "seed," as I called it. I had a seed, not a baby. Not yet. I could not say "baby." With the loving support of my husband, my family, and my awesome doctor, I slowly felt the joy as my tummy grew and I passed each milestone. When I passed 6 weeks I celebrated, since that was when I lost the second pregnancy. When I passed 8 weeks I got a little more spring in my step, since that was when I lost the first pregnancy. Now I was entering unfamiliar territory. I had never made it this far before. Still, I waited for the "other shoe to drop," so to speak. I wanted to be happy, but still fought it. I was not sure what to think. All I could do was take one day at a time. One doctor's appointment at a time. I tried to stay busy so I would not get too overwhelmed with doubt or negativity. It was hard, but I was determined to keep my head up and keep moving forward.

I ALWAYS KNEW IN MY HEART

Eventually, days turned into weeks and weeks turned into three months. Yup, I made it past the threshold! At the 12-week appointment, all was well and perfect. We saw our BABY (no longer a seed) on the ultrasound. It looked exactly like Casper the Ghost! The little head, little arms, everything was super cute!

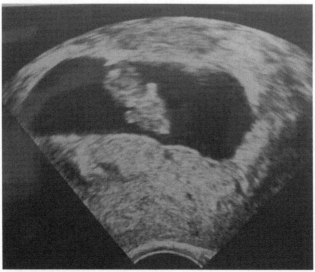

Photo by Ultrasound V.H. Hospital

It was officially a baby and I became flooded with joy. I did it! I reached the summit, saw my ocean view, and could see for miles. This was it! This was our baby and

I felt it deep in my bones. And for the bonus, I could stop doing those suppositories and sleep like a normal person again.

Entering the second trimester was huge for us. We were on our way to parenthood! Wanting to share the joy, I immediately started working on my baby announcement. I recruited my sister to take our photos at a local park. I scoured the internet for cute baby announcement ideas. I got cards printed up so we could mail them to everyone on our Christmas list. I made a Facebook announcement to all my long distant friends and people from my past. I would have shouted it from the rooftops if I could climb up there, **"WE ARE HAVING A BABY!"** All the excitement I kept stuffing down inside was now bubbling up to the surface. Appropriate for this type of celebration, I felt like a human bottle of champagne that had just been opened. We were finally getting the baby who we have been trying for, over the past two-and-a-half years! Here is the announcement we sent out:

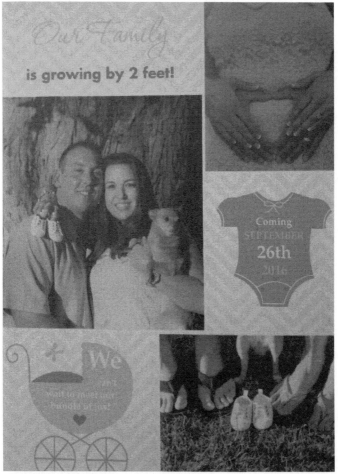

Photos by Jenifer Landis

Even though I *could* find out the sex of my baby early in my pregnancy, my husband and I did not want to know. We did not want a gender reveal party. Nor did we want to paint the nursery pink or blue. To us, it seemed so cliché. I had witnessed my sister *waiting* to learn the sex of her three children on the days they were each born. We wanted that too, even though it was definitely against the norm. And it was quite comical on how upset some of my friends became about it.

"Well, that just isn't fair! I want to know what you are having, don't you?" they would scoff.

I would explain, *"NO, I wanted to wait until the day my baby is born."*

"Then how will I know what to get for your baby? Picking a gift will be too hard if I don't know what you are having!" they would exclaim.

My reply, *"Why don't you get gender neutral colors like yellow, green or gray? You can do it, I believe in you!"*

Hello people! You need to calm down about not knowing the sex of **my** baby. It is my choice, not yours so relax. For thousands of years, babies have been born with parents not knowing. Just because we have the technology does not mean we have to use it. It was funny to see how upset people were. They couldn't stand it that I didn't have the answer. They just couldn't believe *in a million years* that someone could actually wait to know the sex of their baby until it was born. The constant chattering... *"How can this be? How can you hold out for so long? Why, why, why?!"* My thoughts... *"Too bad! You will have to wait with me."* It wasn't even a concern or a difficult thing to do. People have to realize we, as expecting mothers, are free to make our own choices. No, you may not know the sex of my baby before I want you to: my choice. No, you may not touch my pregnant belly, you perfect stranger: my choice. There will be things friends or family may wish so hard for you to do, so they can feel better about it. But, you **can** leave them hanging. All of these things are your choice and no one can tell you differently.

It was a simple thing to make the nursery gray and white. My husband did an outstanding job at painting and putting all the furniture together. Once the baby was born, we would add a pop of blue or pink depending on whether we had a boy or a girl.

A PICTURE IS WORTH A
THOUSAND WORDS

I am lucky enough to have a sister who dabbles in photography. She has hired a professional photographer to capture just about every major milestone in her life. By being the subject of photos many times, she got to watch how they do it. I am guessing this ignited the passion in her a bit. At least enough to go out and purchase a very expensive camera, neck strap and all. So when she offered to do our pregnancy photo shoot, of course I jumped at the chance!

We went to a park and I wore a pink shirt while my husband wore a blue shirt. We did not know what we were having so we thought we could represent both boy and girl. She had us do a lot of cute poses, like up against a tree, sitting on a blanket, standing in the grass, or watching the sunset. I would highly, highly recommend this to every expecting couple because this is such a precious time that you cannot get back. These pictures are so special to us. We used one in my baby announcement and another we blew up onto a canvas that still hangs in our living room. When I scroll through these pictures now, they take me back to that beautiful time in our lives. I'm so thankful we captured those precious moments.

Photo by Jenifer Landis

It is not necessary to hire a professional photographer or use a super fancy camera. Maybe even get a family member or friend to snap a few shots with their phone camera. But do not miss this opportunity, as you may only be pregnant once or twice in your life.

Another thing I have seen done before and I did too, was to take a picture every month to capture the growing baby belly. If you want to do this, take it in the same spot of your house, wear the same dress, and face the same direction. It was cool to see the differences from month to month. You could also set it up as a series and have the photos framed. Our bodies do this amazing thing, and we need to capture every moment to remember how miraculous the experience was, every single part of it!

6 MONTHS   **7 MONTHS**   **8 MONTHS**

Photos by Peter Famiglietti

4

EAT WELL, BE WELL

As my pregnancy progressed, I took my prenatal vitamins, drank lots of water, and ate a healthy diet, rich in vegetables and fruit. I read everything about how to support a healthy baby in the womb through food. There is so much info out there and I found some guidelines that worked for me. Unfortunately, some of the foods *I LOVED* were off limits, due to different reasons that could harm the growth of the baby. No soft cheeses due to possible bacterial infection. UGH! I love me some brie! My husband and I used to have date nights that entailed a glass of wine with some cheese platters. You know the one, with dried cranberries, nuts, sliced fruit, and assorted cheeses. Since my husband went to culinary school, over the past 2 years, he taught me about pairing wine with cheese and I got really into it for the flavors. Now, I wasn't allowed to have wine or cheese. Double BOO!

Also, no fish, no sushi, WHAAAH! Some fish contains high levels of mercury that may harm the brain development of the baby. Not worth the risk, so I avoided it. But it was difficult, since we would go out for sushi once or twice a month. That was the hardest for me. I missed having a magnificent piece of sashimi or a spicy tuna roll. But, I knew the health of my baby, especially THIS miracle rainbow baby, was worth every sacrifice I had to make. I was all in!

For the first three months, I did have "morning sickness." Yet it does not only occur in the morning. For dinner sometimes, my husband would put chicken in the oven. The smell alone made me so nauseous, I wanted to vomit right then and there. Most times I didn't. I only actually threw up twice, but all the other times I would run to the bathroom, dry heave really hard, maybe barf up some bile, or just saliva. Throw up or not, it was gross and still happened to me at all times of the day. Eventually, my husband would cook his chicken far away from me outside on the BBQ. This was the best solution for both of us, since I did not want to take his chicken away from him. Nor did I want to have to smell it.

And then there were the cravings. This is a real thing I tell you! For me, the biggest craving was salty things. I always had a hankering for Lay's Potato Chips. Just a small bag from the gas station. But the real thing that helped me the most, and also curbed the morning sickness, was pickle juice. Yes, the juice! I would stand in front of the refrigerator and drink it straight from the jar. After eating a pickle or two, I would take some major sips of it. My husband would see me and question what the heck I was doing? He hates pickles. After seeing his reaction, I thought, well, maybe drinking this straight up is not the best thing for a growing baby. So I would limit myself to four sips and then put the jar away. But let me tell you, it really did help settle my stomach when I had raging nausea. I have no idea about the science behind *why* it works. Maybe the electrolytes or something. But hey, if you begin to struggle with morning sickness, give this a try.

But the weirdest craving I ever had in the whole pregnancy happened one evening, I was waiting for my husband to come home from work. I had this craving that was so far out in left field, but I had to have it! I called him up and asked if he could bring home Twinkies and Root Beer. I was such a healthy eater he did not even understand where this was coming from. I don't think I have even eaten a Twinkie since I was a child. And root beer? I am not even a soda person. He was completely thrown off. But being the wonderful husband that he is, he brought it home for me and... with vanilla ice cream! He told me if there was root beer involved then *he* for sure wanted a root beer float. I thought, not a bad idea!

There we sat having Twinkies and Root Beer floats. Who would have thought! Certainly not the best choice for a growing fetus, but helping me through this craving crisis was worth it. And the best part was, I got it completely out of my system. I never craved it again and I went right back to my healthy eating for the rest of my pregnancy. I would say this happened around 5 months, and thankfully never happened again. I was okay with my occasional potato chips and pickle juice. Certainly, not every day, but every so often. Cravings are real, so listen to your body and fulfill the cravings so you can get back to your healthy eating.

I ate a lot of organic vegetables, healthy meats (chicken, lean steak) and quality carbohydrates like whole grain bread, whole wheat pasta, and brown rice. I was not worried about counting calories or even portion sizes. I wanted to make sure I was getting the nutrients I needed to grow a tiny human. I avoided sugar and sweets, but I still had my coffee every morning. You are allowed one cup per day and I stuck to it. Although, I switched my sweetener to stevia instead of sugar. During this short but special time in your life, aim to eat as healthy as you're able to. Your little one needs it. You have entered a realm of nine month span of your life where your main focus should be taking care of yourself and the little life you are carrying. Perhaps you used to have a glass of wine every night, or lived by the sea and ate fish daily. Cutting all of this out may seem impossible, but it is a short nine months of your life. And it is the BEST thing you can do for your baby to thrive. Once your baby is born and you are done breastfeeding, you can return to your old ways. Or, you can use this opportunity to make that radical change you have been wishing for. Sometimes it takes a milestone to encourage us to do better, eat better, and be better. Maybe you have been thinking about it for many years but have been struggling. Now is your chance. You only get one chance and only nine months to do it. So go for it! I know you have it in you to eat well and be well.

Fast food was definitely off the table. I was never much of a fast food eater and have not had McDonalds for at least 15 years. If you want to quit McDonald's cold turkey, watch the movie "Super-Size Me" from 2004. It will change the way you think of fast food. I cannot stress how much this stage of your baby's life (pregnancy) depends on *YOU* and how and what you eat. Take this as serious as you can to be the best you can. Your little one is depending on you! If you have a craving (as powerful as they are) I get it. But don't make it a habit. I had one Twinkie and one root beer in the whole nine months and then never had it again. And haven't had it since. If it is a true craving, you will get it out of your system. If you are just trying to use pregnancy as an excuse to eat whatever you want, that is the wrong attitude. Check yourself Momma, your baby is counting on you!

5

MOISTURIZE LIKE NO TOMORROW!

Early on, I read articles about how to avoid getting stretch marks and I am pleased to say I have none! And no cellulite either! This was a huge accomplishment I am so proud of, I am bursting at the seams to share it with YOU. I know so many women struggle in this area, and I can only hope the following information helps you as much as it helped me. It starts as soon as you find out you are pregnant. But even before that, I have always been one to moisturize every time I get out of the shower. This is the key. But I did make the switch from regular lotion to pure cocoa butter. You can see the exact brand I used by flipping to my resource page at the back of this book (page 219). Scan the QR Code and get your cocoa butter today. Because in reality, you needed to start rubbing it on your belly like yesterday! Until your jar of moisturizing goodness arrives, here is exactly how I used the cocoa butter.

I would put it all over my whole body. Paying special attention to my belly and my boobs, since these parts will be growing bigger and bigger soon. I would call it coconut boobs since they became slippery and smelled like coconut. And then I started wearing sports bras. It is a fantastic idea to switch OUT of under-wire bras since your breasts get tender. The wire hurts and you want nothing impeding on the growth of your milk ducts which are rapidly developing to feed your baby. Even though you may only be newly pregnant, your body knows what to do and it happens very early. We, my dear Mommas, are a miracle of nature, able to grow another life inside of us. Do not take this responsibility lightly.

My boobs got very veiny and full. I was already a DD so for me to get even bigger was a little painful. The sports bra kept them in place, stopped them from moving too much while I walked, and limited them from stretching too much in general. Also key, sleep with a sports bra! All my life I never slept with a bra on. I always thought at night was the time for "my girls" to go free. But once you are pregnant, and throughout breastfeeding, you are going to want to support your "puppy girls" so they stay close to your body. Also, keep doing cocoa butter until you complete your breastfeeding journey. As a matter of fact, I still do it today! I did not get stretch marks on my breasts or my belly. Moisturizing is where it's at ladies! And also, drink a TON of water to hydrate from the inside.

HOPE YOU DON'T GET THIS!

Every time there is a low probability of something happening, I end up getting it. The perfect example of this is me getting the PUPPP Rash during pregnancy. What the heck is a PUPPP rash you ask? Yeah, I never heard of it either. PUPPP stands for Pruritic Urticarial Papules and Plaques of Pregnancy. Right? I don't know how to say it either, which is why we use PUPPP. It is a red bumpy rash that appears in different places on your body in the third trimester. Guess how many women get it? Less than 1% of pregnant women. And yup, I got it! It is very itchy and keeps relocating on your body like every week. I had it on my stomach. Then my upper arms. It moved to my thighs and then my butt cheeks. I couldn't seem to stop it from moving around, or get it completely gone either.

Since I love to read articles and do research, I found some home remedies online that were meant to help with the itching. Charcoal soap, which I bought on the web, supposedly helps dry out the rash. I tried drinking tomato juice, which was meant to fight it from the inside by changing my acidity levels to end the rash, or so I read. I tried numerous moisturizers, I did lukewarm oatmeal baths, and wore soft fabrics. All of these were natural cures that sort of soothed the rash temporarily, but not completely. It was a tough last three months of pregnancy. After about two months of this nonsense, I broke down and went to see a dermatologist for some topical medication. This did not harm the baby and I wish I had gone to see a dermatologist sooner! The medicine still did not take the rash completely away, but did soothe the itching and prevent me from wanting to jump out of my skin or scratch until oblivion.

The OBGYN told me the rash might remain well until after I gave birth. Sure enough, it did not fully go away until about a month after my baby was born. I did extensive research to find out WHY I even got PUPPP rash. It is still unknown. First-time mothers can have PUPPP rash since it is their first pregnancy of life or just because their hormones are out of balance. Another theory is, when women are carrying a boy, there is a conflict of cells since he is male and I am female. Well, I had a boy so I am sticking with this theory. But seriously, to this day, I don't know exactly *why* I got it. I am just glad that it is finally in the past! And I hope you don't have to suffer through this either.

6

LET THE NESTING BEGIN

Now that I am fully pregnant, let the nesting begin! What is nesting? In case you haven't heard of this, it is getting everything ready to receive your new baby bundle, and trust me, there is so much! Your car, living room, kitchen, bathroom, the baby's clothes, building new furniture, and decorating the baby room. So, although nine months seems like a long time, it goes by quickly. And I encourage you to use this time wisely to get ready, because there is **so much to do**!

One of the greatest tips I ever received was to make sure I switched to fragrance-free laundry detergent and non-scented dryer sheets. With a new baby coming, who has never been in the world before, you don't want to risk giving him or her a rash from some harsh detergent. I used free and clear laundry detergent (there are multiple brands) and free and clear dryer sheets. Wash all of the baby's bedding, clothes, blankets, and towels beforehand so they can be fresh and ready for newborn skin. Once these items are clean, you can fold them and put them away in that newly built baby dresser in the nursery.

My mom gave me a "baby prepping gem" that I still live by today. And now I even do it for my clothes. Recently, my husband started asking me to do it on his clothes as well! What is it? Cut all the tags out before wearing them. For some odd reason, clothing manufacturers tend to put tags in the weirdest places. Like inside a baby onesie there is a tag at the back of the neck and another one on the side of the hip. How itchy that would be for a baby and they have no way of telling you what is bothering them, which may even keep them up all night. Sorry, but I do not care where the item was made, how to wash it in five languages, or that Inspector #35 checked it. But what I do need is the size!

SIDE NOTE: I made the mistake of cutting out *all* the tags in the first year, so I had no idea what sizes I had. Manufacturers have *just now* started making "back of the neck tags" to be a permanent imprint on the actual material. This is helpful and non-itchy. However, it does become a problem when it starts to wash off and you can no longer see the size anymore. Still, I would rather not know the size and just eyeball it, than have a very itchy, irritated baby on my hands.

Something I love most of all, which especially helped me on this journey, are LISTS! Even present day, I always have some sort of list running to keep me on this fast track of life! I have compiled a list specific to each room so you can follow along the nesting phase and get things completely ready for your new bundle to arrive. I hope these help you simplify!

*All of the products I recommend in the following pages are the **actual products** I used to raise my baby. I wanted a way to make it easier for new Mommas to find everything they need all in one place. When you go to* *buy a stroller, there will be 50 or more choices. When it is time to find a car seat, there are even more varieties. I have narrowed it down for you. Don't feel like you have to do a ton of research or even purchase the ones I am recommending. Just know these products are mom-tested and kid-approved by me and my family. You can see videos of me demonstrating each product on my YouTube channel, and also find links to get yours on my Resource Page at the back of this book. (Page 219)*

THE LIVING ROOM

This is where you will likely be spending the most time on a day-to-day basis. It is close to the kitchen for refueling, probably near a bathroom, and has a comfy place for you to rest, aka sofa. It is important to have all the baby gear you need close by, so you can be prepared and will not have to walk up and down stairs one million times per day. The baby will not care where they are sleeping, whether it is in their crib or the living room. As long as they get sleep! Enter: the Graco Pack-N-Play. This is definitely something you'll want to have on your baby registry.

Honestly, this is the greatest gift you will receive! What is it? A lifesaver! It triples as a sleeping station, changing station, and portable playpen when you travel. We could not live without it! This was the very first baby item we put together in our living room to have it ready as a sleeping place for our baby on the first floor. It was a folding play yard on the bottom for when our little guy grew bigger, and two sections on top were for when he was a newborn. One section was a sleeping cradle that had music, vibrations, and even a night light. The other section had a waterproof padding perfect for changing diapers.

It is also super helpful to have a diaper changing station on every level of your home. The most important part of that station is the Diaper Caddy. It's okay, I didn't know what this was either. A diaper caddy is a box with an easy-carry handle on it to store everything you need for a diaper change. It has compartments, a place for wipes, diapers, rash cream, burping blankets and more!

It is a must have, as you will not want to carry a naked baby up or down stairs while fumbling to get to the only diaper station in your home. So set up at least two. Once you see how many times you will have to change a diaper in a day (maybe 10) then you will be so glad you set yourself up to win at diaper changing!

Living Room Checklist

Pack-n-Play	Put together with changing station
Diaper Caddy	Stocked w/ diapers, wipes, diaper cream
Changing Pad	Best if it is waterproof
Hanging Clothes Organizer	Stocked & all tags removed from clothes
Changes of Clothes	Pre-washed in fragrance free detergent
Onesies	Pre-washed in fragrance free detergent
Shirts, Pants, Socks, & Hats	Pre-washed in fragrance free detergent
Bibs	Pre-washed in fragrance free detergent
Burping Cloths	Pre-washed in fragrance free detergent
Fresh sheet on the sleeping surface	Pre-washed in fragrance free detergent
Blanket	Pre-washed in fragrance free detergent
Sound Machine	Some Pack-n-Plays have music built in
Sheet over couch to catch any spills	Pre-washed in fragrance free detergent
Nipple Shields	Pre-washed in gentle baby dish soap
Nursing Cups	Pre-washed in gentle baby dish soap
Milk Collection Vile	Pre-washed in gentle baby dish soap
Bottles	Pre-washed in gentle baby dish soap
Breast Pump	Plugged in, all parts pre-washed

YOUR HOSPITAL TRAVEL BAG

Ok ladies! This is one of the most important things you can have ready for the day of delivery. No one knows when their water will break or where they will be. (I certainly did not know and there is NO WAY to predict it either.) Having my hospital bag ready gave me great comfort, peace of mind, and accomplishment. I had mine ready and in the car about three months before my due date. All the while leading up to it, I kept nudging my husband to get his bag ready. And he would tell me, "Yeah, yeah, I will." Whelp, he never did. So he had to wear the same underwear for three days in the hospital. Bah Ha! Sorry, Honey! ☺

Keep in mind you will pack away clothes that you do not wear regularly. Clothes and beauty products you will not miss having available for the next two months. If you only have one toothbrush, buy another so you can have the new one packed away. If you only have one shampoo, make or get a travel size for your bag. Just know this: you will have to leave the house or wherever you are in a moment's notice, with NO TIME to think about anything but the baby.

Here is my compilation of what made me comfortable in the hospital for three days. Keep in mind, they do let the Mommas shower there, but not your partner.

Travel Bag for Hospital Checklist

Your Favorite Shampoo	Travel size
Conditioner	Travel size
Body Wash or Soap	Travel size
Loofa	In zip bag to catch the drips
Cocoa Butter	Start rubbing on tummy now!
Face Products	Moisturizer, eye make-up remover
Toothbrush	Get a travel toothbrush
Toothpaste	Travel size
Any Medications You Currently Take	
Vitamins	No need to bring big bottles. Just bring a small zip bag with enough for 3 days.
Small Make-Up bag (there will be pictures!)	Keep it basic, like 3 items: lip gloss, mascara, and eye shadow
Hairbrush	Travel size
Rubber Bands: I wore braids	They are comfy & easy to sleep on
Four changes of clothes	You will be there three days but you'll want something fresh to go home in
Underwear	Bring 7-8 pairs
Nursing Bras or sports bras	Remember, no under-wire
Comfy Stretchy Pants	No jeans here, trust me!
Loose Shirts and Tank Tops	Both long and short sleeve
Pajamas	Something comfy, pants are best
Zip-able Sweatshirts or open long sleeves	The hospital is kept at a cold temperature
Socks or slippers	Something washable you can walk around the hospital in
Robe	I did not pack mine & I wish I had!
Snacks (dry goods)	Things that keep well in the car for several months like trail mix, nuts, granola bars
Multiple Outfits for the Baby	There will be spills and drips!
One Nice Baby Outfit for Taking Pictures	We brought both gender outfits since we didn't know what we were having
Diapers and Wipes	The hospital does provide these but I wanted to get used to how my diapers worked

YOUR CAR

Thankfully, my husband knew how to install the baby car seat without a problem. We chose the Graco Snugride Snuglock 35 Elite Infant Car Seat because it was fully functional to take your baby places with you. As a new Momma, trust me, you and your baby will be doing lots of errands together. This car seat system simplified my life in ways I didn't know I needed. There is even a special insert in case your baby is a preemie or just extra small. The biggest bonus of this car seat was how I could just continue about my day and not worry if my baby falls asleep or not. I could literally take him wherever I needed to go, asleep or awake, it didn't matter. This car seat could accommodate every situation. Yes, this one was a little on the pricey side, but worth every penny since it offered me amazing convenience I could not find with other car seat systems.

Another HUGE selling point for me was the fact that the entire seat can click out of your car, and into a stroller frame. Meaning, if the baby falls asleep while you are driving to your first errand (which is often) you can just click the whole seat out of the car, sleeping baby included, and click them into some wheels and roll the baby into your first store. No need to unbuckle a seat belt, try to pick him up, or transfer him to a different apparatus while possibly waking him up in the process. (As they say, "Never wake a sleeping baby." TRUE!) With this system, you don't have to ever wake your baby. This was amazing! As long as you get the stroller compatible with this car seat. For me, it was the Graco Modes Click Connect Stroller.

But wait, there's more! Not only did this car seat click in and out with ease, but it saved us from having to buy more than one. What am I even talking about? Well, if you have a car, and your partner has a car, it would be super annoying to buy two *separate* car seats. That's twice the price. But, what is even more troublesome is if you have only one car seat, but still two cars, having to remember to switch it back and forth between both cars. God forbid your partner leaves the house with the car seat in the back, and you have to take the baby to a doctor's appointment in 10 minutes. You become stuck and have no way of driving your baby because you have only one car seat and it is not in your car! I did not want to put myself in these situations if I could avoid it. What makes this Graco system super convenient, is all you need to do is to buy two bases. Each system has a base that stays permanently buckled into the car with the actual seat belts of that car. Instead of buying two separate car seats for twice the price, just buy two bases. One for your car and one for your partner's. That way, every time you leave the house with the baby bundle in his car seat, you can just click him into the base that remains set up in the vehicle. Fantastic! I am so grateful my husband thought of this solution. I just had to share it with you too!

And get an additional base if you are a single or working Momma and will have a regular caretaker for your baby. Perhaps Grandma, an In-law, or babysitter will also be driving your baby around. You won't have time to mess with installing the car seat, or the extra expenses to buy an extra car seat for this person.

A friend of mine told me this story: *"I can't tell you how many times I was running late because my mother-in-law forgot to put their car seat in the car for my son. I had to remove mine and reinstall it in their* car. Plus, she didn't have the strength to tighten the seat as much as it needed to be, so I always had to do it. We'll be buying extra bases this time around!"

Keeping your baby safe in the car is super important. But driving safely is also key, and having peace of mind that your baby is okay will make you a better driver. You will want to see your baby while he is in the backseat. This can do a lot for how you drive, either make it or **brake** it (see what I did there?) If you cannot see the baby you will wonder the entire drive if he is awake, asleep, or even breathing. There is a backseat baby mirror made specifically for this purpose. Get one! Or maybe two if your baby will be riding in more than one vehicle. I had one in my car and one in my husband's as well. Don't forget the caretaker, or whoever else will be driving your precious cargo. Maybe you need three of them! I speak from experience on this one. We did not install the mirror that faces the baby so we can see him from the front seat. Keep in mind, your baby will face the backseat. So there is no way to see their little face while you are driving without the baby backseat mirror. Never have I ever seen my husband drive so slow in my life! I think he did 45 MPH on the freeway where the speed limit is 65 MPH. I kept turning around to check on our baby to make sure: I had fastened the seat belt, he had his toy, and he had a blanket, was he awake, or did he need anything else. We were both nervous wrecks taking him home from the hospital that first day. Put the mirror in well before you leave to give birth in the hospital. You will want to have it in place while you are driving home for the first time.

Car Checklist

Car Seat	Assembled and installed, rear facing
Baby Mirror for the Backseat	Out of package and installed
Diaper Bag	Stocked w/ diapers, wipes, & rash cream
Burping Cloths	Pre-washed in fragrance free detergent
Pacifiers	Bring more than one since the baby will drop it on the dirty car floor

KITCHEN

Have a sanitary station where you will wash and dry your bottles and nursing equipment. This needs to be in its own section away from where you will prepare raw food (chicken, meats, onions, etc.). Also, not too close to the stove or oven as most bottle-feeding equipment is plastic and can melt. This is something you can do ahead of time before your baby arrives. Everything needs to be washed before you feed your little bundle. No use trying to do all of this while the baby is crying and waiting for you to feed them! Do it early while you have time.

One of my favorites on this list is the Green Grass Drying rack. When I saw this, I immediately registered for it, as I thought it was the cutest thing out there. It is an adorable drying rack for all your breastfeeding needs. And it keeps everything handy in one section of your countertop.

Kitchen Checklist

Delicate Dish Soap (non-scented)	For cleansing baby gear & utensils
Sponge (separate from your dish sponge)	To clean baby gear & keep sanitary
Plastic Green Grass Drying Rack	Away from your normal drying rack
Pacifiers	Orthodontist approved so no overbite
Bottle Nipples	Washed and ready to go
Nipple Shields	Washed and ready to go
Nursing Cups	Washed and ready to go
Milk Collection Vile	Washed and ready to go

YOUR BATHROOM

You will be sent home from the hospital with a "Care Kit" to take care of your aching vagina. Yup! You heard it here first. You will have damage. For me, my son's head was too big, so I had to get cut to allow him to pass. And then stitches. Oh yes, my dear ladies, it is like a crime scene down there, so follow the instructions they give you. Partners, just be aware, that you might not have any action with her for about 6 weeks. Plus, you probably won't want to see it either. The best thing you can do for her is offer her help through the door of the bathroom, ask if she needs more warm water or a towel. Give her an arm or a shoulder to help hobble back to the couch or bed. This is where the genuine love that you have for her, and the baby she just gifted you, shines through. When my husband took care of my crying baby or did a simple diaper change, it meant the world to me! Even making her a snack without her asking for one, can be huge! Step up, partners. Look at what she just did for you.

Although the hospital sends you home with a decent amount of products in your "Care Kit" you will need to stop somewhere to get more. A day or two after we were home and settled, we took an outing to the pharmacy to get more supplies. He specifically parked in the back of the parking lot so I could nurse my baby in private. I sent my husband into the store with a list, while I got ready to bust out my boob for some feeding time. I will never forget it because a few rows down in this totally empty parking lot, a car pulled up, like five spaces away. And some high school kids hopped out to sit on the hood of their car and smoke some weed. Great! Now I cannot open my window for fresh air and I have to take extra care to cover up so these dudes don't sneak a peek. It was my first-time nursing in public, but I managed to get the job done. As new Mommas we have to overcome, and I did it. You will too!

The hospital "should" send you home with a little plastic insert for your toilet. This is meant to be filled with warm water to sit in and promote healing. Do this several times per day. I always enjoyed doing this right before a shower, as it tends to get messy and drip all over the place when you stand up. Also, a squirt bottle to fill with warm water to spray your undercarriage. You should do this after every time you go to the bathroom. If the hospital does not provide you with these items, be sure to get them. It is so important to keep the area flushed with warm water to prevent infection.

Bathroom Checklist for Momma

Maxi Pads	The biggest you can find!
Cooling Spray	You will want to spray directly on your aching muffin
Gauze	To lay across your maxi pad
Tuck's Witch Hazel Pads	To lay across your maxi pad. The witch hazel has a cooling effect and soothes.

Around the House for Momma

Doggy Pee Pee Pads	These work great to protect furniture
Blue Gel Ice packs in Freezer	Wrap them in a washcloth then put it right in your underwear. It soothes so much!

YOUR BEDROOM

We decided early on to have our baby sleep in his own space and not in the bed with us. There were numerous discussions about this and we felt it was best for all of us. Also, after I read an article or two about SIDS or the possibility of rolling on top of your baby during your sleep, that scared us enough to not even try. My husband is a big man and I tend to flail my arms and legs in my sleep. So, neither of us wanted to harm the baby.

No judgement on those who choose differently. Baby cuddles are so mushy and delicious. I could see how heartwarming it would be to have them all night long and never let them end. But from what I hear, once the baby sleeps with you, it is a *very* hard habit to break. I never wanted to have fights about this with my husband or worry about trying to get a sleeping baby, toddler, or pre-teen out of my own bed. And I certainly didn't want a baby in my bed to affect our sex life. Teaching my baby about having his own place to sleep started in our household the day we brought him home.

We had our baby sleep in a bassinet at the base of our bed. This was truly special because all my nieces and nephews got to use this same one. It has been passed down the family line. Now it is my baby's turn to snuggle up in this bassinet. He could have his own little bed, free from two sleeping steamrollers. This is the set up you will need to get ready in your room:

Your Bedroom Checklist

Baby Bassinet	For the baby to be close by for feedings
Bassinet Sheets On	Pre-washed in fragrance free detergent
Diaper Changing Station	Stocked w/ diapers, wipes, & rash cream
Pacifiers	Buy several to keep throughout the house
Sound Machine	Borrowed from the nursery
Fresh Pajamas	Pre-washed in fragrance free detergent
Swaddle Cloths	Pre-washed in fragrance free detergent
Burping Cloths	Pre-washed in fragrance free detergent
Rocking Chair Glider w/ Ottoman	Borrowed from the nursery
Side Table by Rocking Chair	To hold all your nursing gear
Book or Tablet	This will help pass the time and keep you awake while feeding

GETTING THE NURSERY READY

Ever since I found out I was pregnant, we knew we did not want to learn the gender of the baby. So, I googled "gender neutral nursery ideas." There is a plethora of creativity out there! We looked at so many adorable themes. It took us about 3 months to decide which one to go with. I would save pictures on my phone of different nursery ideas and furniture that I liked. I also started taking notes on where to buy these items. It is a great way to get your thoughts in order and narrow it down. We decided on gray and white as the base. Then later, when we found out what we were having, we could accent it with blue or pink pillows, curtains, stuffed animals, crib sheets, etc. Once the decision was made, my husband was on top of his game on this one. My baby was due in September and he had the nursery designed and painted by July! He wanted the paint to be completely dry and cured so there would be no fumes for our new baby. This was something I *never* would have thought of. Once it was painted, he started putting all the furniture together. For us, it only consisted of 3 items:

Baby Room Furniture Checklist	
Dresser with Drawers	This doubled as our changing table
Crib w Waterproof Mattress Pad	Be sure to get waterproof for diaper leaks!
Rocking Chair Glider w/ Ottoman	Perfect for nursing, snuggles, & rocking your baby to sleep in

We chose all white furniture since it went so well with our gender neutral theme. Let me make one distinction here: When shopping for furniture, you will notice two types of furniture: a changing table and a dresser. These are two different pieces. I scoured the internet and I did not find a combination of these two pieces together in one. After much research, I chose *NOT* to get a changing table as a piece of furniture because after two or three years, once the baby was out of diapers, there would be no need for this piece. Changing tables have permanent wooden sides built into the top of the table so the baby will not roll away. Any responsible parent knows not to leave the baby on the table unattended. I opted for a dresser with a changing pad on top. The changing pad was soft, like a firm pillow and had sides to assist with the baby not rolling. Same thing though, I never left him unattended while changing a diaper. That is why it was so important to have everything you need, fully stocked within arm's reach for diaper changing. Then, once your baby is grown and out of diapers, you can remove the changing pad and they can have a normal dresser throughout their childhood and teen years. In the long run, purchasing a dresser will save you from having to buy two pieces of furniture over time.

You will definitely want to invest in a Diaper Genie. What is a Diaper Genie, you ask? Only one of the favorite baby items ever! It is a contraption that keeps the diaper stink at bay. No matter how bad of a diaper blowout your baby has, or what consistency it may be, firm, goopy, soupy or diarrhea, the Diaper Genie can handle it all! If you throw poopy diapers in a regular trash can, you WILL be sorry! Be sure to get your Diaper Genie right away.

Baby Room Checklist

Paint First	At least two months ahead of time so the paint can cure with no fumes for baby
Build Furniture	Crib, dresser, glider, and ottoman
Baby Clothes	Pre-washed in fragrance free detergent
Burping Cloths	Pre-washed in fragrance free detergent
Blankets	Pre-washed in fragrance free detergent
Swaddle Blankets	Pre-washed in fragrance free detergent
CUT ALL TAGS FROM ALL THE CLOTHING	DO THIS NOW & NO SCRAMBLING LATER
Fold Everything	Put away in newly built dresser
Waterproof Changing Pad	Install on top of dresser using screw straps
Put Changing Pad Cover on Pad	Pre-washed in fragrance free detergent
Black Out Curtains on Windows	A dark room is a happy baby room
Sound Machine	Removed from box, plugged in & tested
Baby Monitor	Installed & working
Waterproof Mattress Pad on Crib	Pre-washed in fragrance free detergent
Crib Sheets Put on Crib Mattress	Pre-washed in fragrance free detergent
Diaper Caddy Fully Stocked	Diapers, Wipes, & diaper rash cream
Baby Body Lotion	Delicate brand made for babies
Baby Hairbrush	Gentle bristles for newborn scalp
Nail Clipper	TIP: Clip nails while baby is asleep, It is so much less stressful for you, Momma
Baby Mobile to Match Your Theme	Hang above the crib or changing area
Diaper Genie	Put together with refills in place

A BATHROOM FOR THE BABY

If you have more than one bathroom, consider yourself lucky. I recommend making the one closest to the nursery for the baby. This will make it much easier for bath time and take them right into their room to enjoy all that you have prepared. You want your baby to feel they have their own space. After all, you put a lot of thought and hard work into this room. Might as well make the most of it.

Bathroom for Baby Checklist

Baby Shampoo	A gentle brand for babies
Baby Conditioner	A gentle brand for babies
Baby Body Wash	A gentle brand for babies
Baby Bathtub with Hammock Insert	This held my squirmy baby in place so I could get a good cleaning in
Washcloths	Pre-washed in fragrance free detergent
Hooded Baby Towels	Pre-washed in fragrance free detergent
Bath Cup	To pour over baby's head & body to rinse
Bathtub Mat with Temperature Gauge	This helped me make a bath not too hot
Sanitary Station to Clean All Your Breastfeeding Gear	Gentle dish soap, sponge, clean cloth to lay them out to dry

After a bath, in *their* bathroom, it is easy to take them right to the changing table to dress them. That way *you* will not break your back and *they* can enjoy looking at their future room.

All of the lists I provide in this book are available to print on my website. Use the password: **Nesting**

Visit **https://www.myrockerbeez.com/lists**

7

GRAB ALL THE KNOWLEDGE
YOU CAN, WHERE YOU CAN

When I was about six months pregnant, my husband
and I started taking prenatal classes offered by the
hospital where I was going to give birth. After taking
the tour of the hospital, seeing the delivery room,
recovery area and nursery, we felt pretty good about
our choice of hospitals. Since I was a first-time
mother, I wanted to be as prepared as possible. (I am
such a planner in my life anyway, so the more
preparation I could do, the better). Together we

enrolled in a 6-week childbirth course. We learned about what to expect, all of the options they offered, epidurals, C-sections, what happens in case of an emergency, building your birth plan, and so much more! To me, this was so perfect since I wanted all the knowledge I could get about this new adventure. Preparation is the key!

There were 12 couples in the class and we were probably the oldest and also the furthest away from the due date. The classes started in June and my due date was September 26th. Most women were due in July or August. But no big deal. I liked having the information early and took notes so I would not forget these valuable gems I was about to learn. I was 41 and it seemed like everyone else was in their twenties, just out of college, or early thirties. I was not even worried about being the oldest. I felt like "I got this." I am still not sure *why* I felt this way. Perhaps it was because I had more grey hair than everyone else. Or if being older gave me more wisdom and life experience than these young whippersnappers! What mattered most was this class worked out extremely well for me, in helping me feel prepared, instead of going into the childbirth experience blind. If you have access to anything like this in your town or hospital where you plan to give birth, TAKE IT! One-thousand percent, take the class!

We went around the room and introduced ourselves. We all came from different backgrounds, cultures, age groups, and hometowns, but here we are, being brought together by childbirth. Since it was a two-hour class every week for six weeks, toward the end you get to know one another a little bit. Lots of times there were questions thrown out there so you could learn a little bit more about someone's personality by the end of the course. Not that I became close friends with any of these people, or anything, but it was good to have chit chat on bathroom breaks and trade stories. I felt this overwhelming sense of community with a bunch of "strangers" but we were all brought together by our unborn babies. It was comforting to see other women at the exact stage as me, waddling around with their big bellies and know I am not alone in this.

When we covered the subject of "drugs" or "no drugs" the instructor used an interesting exercise. She passed out this piece of paper and asked us to circle which one fit our needs best. Since her page was property of the hospital and copyrighted, I could not print the actual page in my book. So this is my version of me paraphrasing so you get the general idea. Most hospitals use them in their curriculum, so pay close attention when you get yours at your birthing class.

On a scale of 1-10 circle your pain threshold:

#10　I have a high tolerance for pain and I want to do natural childbirth as much as possible. I plan to work through all the labor pain and wish to receive absolutely NO DRUGS if everything remains safe for the baby.

#9　I can tolerate most pain and want to have a natural childbirth. My tolerance is about a 9 but I am not wanting to go full throttle to a 10 and beyond. I hope the pain does not get out of hand because I don't want to take pain medicine, if I can help it.

#8　My pain threshold is pretty-strong. I can tolerate most things, but not as powerfully as someone who is a 10. I would be open to other medicines to ease some pain before going full epidural. I would like all options presented to me and would most likely do a mixture of light drugs and natural childbirth. I would like to avoid the epidural if possible.

#7   Natural childbirth is important to me, and since I am a 7, I am confident I can do it. I know there is a "point of no return" for the epidural. I would like to be notified when that is, so I can have the option to choose, in that moment or not. I want to push through all the way, but I also want to have all my options open.

#6   I can tolerate most pain fairly well. I have heard about labor so I am leery about this venture. But I do want to give natural childbirth a good, honest try. I want to stay in natural labor for at least two hours. I am not sure if I can go all the way, and I want to have all the drugs available in case I might need them.

#5   I would like to attempt labor but just knowing the epidural is there as a safety net is comforting to me. Natural childbirth is important to me, but not if it starts to hurt too much. I may want to have it if, midway through, I realize I just cannot do it.

#4   I choose 4 as my pain number since I can handle a medium amount of pain but not quite up to a 5. I feel somewhat confident I can do labor, but I want to put a time limit on it. I will give labor a chance for one hour. If it hurts me too much, I want to have an epidural.

#3   I would like to give labor a try, even though I am pretty sure I won't be able to do it as I sit here right now. I am willing to try going natural for about a half an hour. After that, if it is too much, give me the pain meds!

#2   I don't like pain. Things hurt me very easily. I will try natural labor for about 10 minutes but I already can tell you, it will probably be too much for me. I would want the epidural on hand, standing close by, to numb me after 5 minutes.

#1   I have NO tolerance for pain. I want an epidural as soon as my water breaks. I do not want to feel any amount of labor or any amount of pain. I just cannot handle it.

I circled 10 as I was wanting to do natural labor in the strongest possible way. I did not want ANY drugs or epidural if I could help it.

Then we went around the room and each shared what we circled. Lo and behold, one other woman and me, were only ones who circled #10. Everyone else circled #1, #2, or #3. They all wanted drugs. Ten out of twelve couples wanted an epidural or some type of pain medicine. This was very eye opening to me. One woman even asked if she could schedule her C-Section. This way they could just take the baby out and she wouldn't have to push. The instructor said they do not allow the scheduling of C-Sections "just because." C-Sections are used for an emergency and the first route is to always try natural birth. Regardless, every woman has the choice to do what they will with their bodies and babies. I knew I wanted to at least try to be all natural, like my sister, and my mother.

Let's get back to the only other couple that matched my number. Well, they were a little further on the spectrum than I was. At one point, they asked the instructor if they could bring the placenta home with them. They could, they just needed a doctor's note and to fill out a form. It's important to mention, in some cultures it is customary to eat the placenta to replenish the nutrients lost during childbirth. Eeeek! Not my cup of tea but to each their own. This couple was going for the most natural birth plan I have ever heard of. I was kind of wondering why they did not choose to give birth in a pool of water or their home, and instead were going to this hospital. They reminded me of my sister and how she gave birth at a birthing center, not a hospital, so she did have the "pool of water" option. And I think she used it. I was headed in that direction, until I had my first miscarriage. Come to think of it, my sister did something with her placenta as well. I think she had it sent somewhere to get dried out and turned into vitamin capsules. She was a vegan at the time, so perhaps she felt the need to replenish herself after childbirth. For me, a fat juicy steak would serve me just fine. That is the beauty of the birthing journey. We can choose our own path of what works for our personal choice as a soon-to-be Momma and our baby.

There are many options for doing things with the placenta after you gave birth. But it did not interest me one bit. After giving birth, the doctor always asks if you want to see the placenta. I had to prepare myself on how to answer this question. I made sure my husband would tell them, "NO WAY!" I can't even bear to watch some gory stuff on a simple show like "Bones" or "ER," so why would I want to see my gross afterbirth? HARD PASS! More power to those who want (or are able) to give birth in their home, in a pool of water or a birth center. They truly go against the norm and I have to hand it to them, BRAVO! I hold a high respect for you, Mom Warriors. For thousands of years, women have given birth under trees, by the river, no drugs, and no other options. That was not my choice anymore, as I wanted all the emergency equipment there in the hospital in case something went wrong. Especially now, with my history of two miscarriages. I needed to find a happy medium between birthing in a hospital (just in case) and maintaining my natural status, although, not in a field of flowers somewhere.

8

A BIRTH PLAN: WHAT IS IT, AND WHY YOU NEED ONE

The class continued and after we learned all the options of giving birth, they asked us to write a birth plan. I didn't know what it was. I actually googled it to see what some people put on their birth plan. I learned a lot and picked what I wanted. I tried to think of things that would help me relax. Music, dim lighting, my favorite snacks. (I later learned I needed an empty stomach, yet I still snuck a few bites of snacks anyway. More on this later.) The instructor told us this hospital was pretty good about following the birth plan as closely as possible. I thought this was excellent! Apparently, some hospitals out there don't really care. We were very lucky! Me being the planner that I am, typed and printed out three copies of my birth plan and put them in sheet protectors: one for me, one for the nursing staff, and one to post on the wall. These went right into my hospital bag, which, as you already know, was packed and put in the car, months before my delivery date. This was my Birth Plan.

Baby Famiglietti Birth Plan

FATHER: PETER   **MOTHER: BARBIE**

1) No feathers on pillows or bedding. I (mother) am highly allergic.

2) Music, dim lighting, and relaxation

3) No visitors in the labor room, please. Just husband as the coach.

4) Ability to move freely around the room and hallways. I want to keep moving and let gravity do some of the work.

5) DO NOT OFFER DRUGS or pain medicine to mother. Natural birth is MOST important (unless medically necessary for an emergency.)

6) I'd like to hold my baby skin to skin, as soon as possible, and for as long as possible.

7) I would love to hold my baby for 1 hour after birth and possibly breastfeed during this time.

8) Please clean and do any tests needed while I am holding my baby immediately after birth.

9) We request delayed cord-cutting to get the most cord blood into our baby after birth.

10) Dad will cut the cord when it is time. Hopefully after 8 minutes.

11) Dad will go with our baby everywhere throughout the hospital.

12) DO NOT OFFER pacifiers or bottles. BREASTFEEDING ONLY!

13) We would like ALL procedures and medications explained to us BEFORE they are performed or administered to our baby.

14) No multiple vaccines or shots after birth except Vitamin K and Hepatitis B.

15) We are doing a delayed vaccine schedule with our pediatrician.

16) If our baby is a boy, we request circumcision before we leave the hospital.

After much research, I put these things on my Birth Plan because they became most important to me. I realized that sometimes, nurses are on autopilot and follow the American Standard of care for every newborn. As a mother, you can deny some of these things and do not have to be subjected to the mainstream.

1) No feathers on pillows or bedding. I (mother) am highly allergic!

When my nursing staff read this, they laughed out loud and you could hear an unusual cackle throughout the halls of the delivery floor. One of them even said, "What do you think this is, the Ritz?" I guess it never occurred to me. This was not a hotel, it was a hospital. I had nothing to worry about, as far as feathers were concerned. I am not sure if any hospital has feathers in the U.S. but this one did not. Ha! The joke is on me, I guess!

2) Music, dim lighting, and relaxation.

I wanted to have a peaceful birthing experience, and control as many aspects of it as possible. Environment was one of them. I highly recommend a hospital tour so you have a sense of the room, what it looks like and the layout. You can then figure what will help you in that room to stay calm and confident. That's why I asked for dim lighting and calming music. Each delivery room has a TV but I didn't want it on. I am not a big TV watcher and the last thing I wanted was the news, or some dramatic show on TV to raise my heart rate and stress me out before I gave birth.

3) No visitors in the labor room, please. Just my husband as the coach.

I wanted to preserve this private sanctuary for the focus and togetherness of my husband and me. Doctors and nurses can come and go but, no family or friends. Plus, I knew my legs would be wide open for all to see my "everything," and I didn't want to broadcast my lady parts to the entire world.

4) Ability to move freely around the room and hallways. I want to keep moving and let gravity do some of the work.

It was important to ask for the ability to move around. Some hospitals rarely allow it unless you ask. This was one thing I learned from my sister having given birth outside of the hospital. Her doula allowed her to move about the birthing center during labor. She could lay on the bed, sit in a chair, get on all fours, or walk around. Gravity encourages the baby toward the birth canal, so I made sure to include this on my birth plan. I alternated between standing and sitting, laying on my back, or on my side. It helped to have this freedom instead of being stuck in one position. Labor was uncomfortable so letting the staff know ahead of time was extremely helpful.

5) DO NOT OFFER drugs or pain medicine to mother. Natural birth is MOST important (unless medically necessary for an emergency).

Even though I stated it clearly in my birthing plan about not offering me any pain killers or medicine, the nurse kept asking me every hour if I wanted an epidural. I guess they have to, as it surely is another way the hospital can make money, in my opinion. And there was a certain "point of no return" when I could no longer have an epidural if this point is passed. Still, I did not want it and by me having this request in my Birthing Plan, the nurse probably only asked me every hour, instead of every 15 minutes!

6) I'd like to hold my baby skin to skin, as soon as possible, and for as long as possible.

After reading many articles on this, it became very apparent to me the importance of this simple act. Your baby has been listening to your voice ever since it developed ears. Having the chance to meet you face to face and feel your touch would be the same thing as you meeting your Maker. It's a single precious moment, which you can never capture again. Soak it in, Mommas! Skin to skin contact allows the baby to form the first bond of life with you and imprint on you. Just like when the baby duck follows whoever they see first, is called imprinting. Your baby imprints on you. Partners can do skin to skin contact on their chest to bond too. After you have breastfed, of course. Mommy's bond is first and foremost. Sorry, partners! Some babies may not open their eyes for a few days, but when they do see you with their own eyes, for the first time, it is magic. You will not want to miss it! Be sure to put skin to skin contact in your Birth Plan, because some hospitals whisk the baby away to get him or her cleaned up. Try to give birth and then put your baby right on your chest to bond.

7) I would love to hold my baby for 1 hour after birth and possibly breastfeed during this time.

Each hospital has a lactation consultant and they will come to teach you how to latch. I did want to hold him for a good long time, to bond more, and he sure did come out hungry. It was a great way to guide the hospital staff, so they knew I wanted to breastfeed immediately. There was a lot of hustle and bustle during childbirth -- cleaning up, checking yours and the baby's vitals, measurements, and more. Sometimes the staff needs a guide so they don't forget time is of the essence!

8) Please clean and do any tests you need to do while I am holding baby immediately after birth.

This was my wish as I could not wait to meet my little one! Nine months of growing, rubbing my belly, talking to him, this magical miracle my body was creating. I did not want to lose a moment after he came into this world. However, it was the one request they did not meet. Unfortunately, they whisked him away from me to clean him, weigh him, and measure his stuff. Daddy was by his side taking pictures off my left shoulder. I was actually okay with how this went because I seriously needed to catch my breath and regroup after all the pushing and prodding. It was a span of about 15 minutes and then I held my little bundle in my arms, wrapped in the hospital blanket. Either way, we still got to meet. Delayed or not. The Birthing Plan was a guideline. It may or may not be perfect, but at least you put it on paper, and attempt to fulfill your wishes.

9) We request delayed cord-cutting to get the most cord blood into our baby after birth.

There was a lot of excellent information I read about this. There is an incredible amount of nutrient dense, "once-in-a-lifetime" vitamins and healthy goodness alive in the umbilical cord. If the cord gets cut or clamped immediately after the child is born, you miss out on all that good stuff. Capture all the possible nutrients you can, or at least try to!

10) Dad will cut the cord when it is time. Hopefully after 8 minutes.

It was a proud and beautiful moment when Dad cut the cord for his own baby. I wanted this for him. Since I was the one who carried the baby, I ate all the good food to build him, I felt each and every kick, and I was the one who gave birth. Dad had such a minor role in all of this, so I tried my best to include him. I saw the gleam in his eyes when he got to cut it. I took a picture and it was another priceless moment added to our birth-story collection. Also, 8 minutes seems to be the sweet spot of how long it takes the placental blood to make it from placenta to your baby outside the womb.

11) Dad will go with our baby everywhere throughout the hospital.

This was very, very key for us as new parents. My sister taught me this one, as she had her husband in "hawk- mode" after their first son was born. She had a complication during pregnancy at the birth center with her doula, so she ended up in the hospital. She learned a lot of "what not to do" by getting thrown into the hospital system against her wishes. But, all things fall to the wayside, once your baby's birth becomes complicated. Our dreams of floating on a cloud to Yoga music, so the baby can have his own soft landing on a cloud floating by, can be ripped away at the seams, if something goes slightly wrong. Just prepare for this scenario, too. Not everything always goes perfectly, and I can guarantee you that it won't be exactly as you anticipate.

My sister designated her husband to follow the baby all around the hospital, to supervise the staff, and learn about all that needed to be done with their new bundle, only a few hours old. He asked a lot of questions to understand what they were about to do before they were about to do it. A perfect example of this, a nurse was about to give their baby a pacifier full of medicine. They were adamant about not giving the baby a pacifier for any reason. That was their path. So as a new dad, my brother-in-law stopped the nurse and asked her why she was about to give him the pacifier?

The nurse replied, *"Oh, well we are about to give him a vaccine and some Vitamin K, as a shot in his foot. The medicine on the pacifier will numb it, so he won't feel it and he won't cry."*

My brother-in-law replied, *"Well, just let him cry and feel it! We don't want to introduce pacifiers ever and don't want to put random medicine in our newborn baby with a perfect immune system. We will pass on the pacifier, just give him the shot."*

And they did. The baby got the shot, he cried, and he was okay in the end. Why give medicine when it is completely unnecessary? (In my opinion.)

I found this as an interesting exchange and my brother-in-law told us it was a good idea to designate my husband to be our baby's "bulldog." And have him follow our baby and the nurse's staff around the hospital everywhere they took him. I agreed, since we were new parents, and didn't know what to expect. We did talk about everything well beforehand to make sure our intentions were clear and consistent. If the staff started to do something we didn't want done, we said something. Just know as a parent, you can veto anything.

12) DO NOT OFFER pacifiers or bottles. BREASTFEEDING ONLY!

Many articles I read suggested not introducing anything other than the breast, if your main intention is to breastfeed. Especially during the first few days after birth. It took a little grit and muscle to sometimes fight the nursing staff, just as the example above reigns true. Though some hospitals are perfectly accommodating and listen to your requests, with no problems. Others may not. It is up to you to put your wishes on paper, before the little one is even here, so everyone, including the staff, can be up to speed on what is about to go down.

13) We would like ALL procedures and medications explained to us BEFORE they are performed or administered to our baby.

This fell under the "bulldogging" of following the baby all around the hospital while Momma took a rest. Keep an eye on your newest treasure, partners. Some procedures were unnecessary. We did not want a ton of medicine pumped into our brand-new baby. I worked hard to eat well, avoid dangerous food, got lots of rest, and grew him to the BEST of my ability. I wanted him to stay as natural as possible in his first few days, and for life!

14) No multiple vaccines or shots after birth except vitamin K and Hepatitis B.

Yes, much research brought me to this conclusion. Babies are born with low Vitamin K* due to blood loss and transitioning from the womb to the real world. Their first time becoming detached from their mother's blood supply creates a large drop in Vitamin K. My husband and I were fine with this shot to boost the baby's Vitamin K, right after passing through the birth canal. Hepatitis B, a dangerous disease for a newborn to contract, was also a no-brainer for us. He was given this after birth, as well. But that was it! Most hospitals want to offer a slew of shots, vaccines, boosters, etc. but the risks outweighed the reward. It took much research on my own to determine what was best for my baby. I encourage you to do the same.

*https://women.texaschildrens.org/blog/dispelling-myths-vitamin-k-injections-newborns

15) We are doing a delayed vaccine schedule with our pediatrician.

Everyone has their path, and getting on a delayed vaccine schedule with the pediatrician later, was **very** important to us. My baby would receive his vaccines at a later date. I didn't feel he needed them all at birth. Two was my maximum, which would yield very few side effects. As a Momma, it is up to you to do the research, talk to other Moms, and make informed decisions for your child. You will learn as a new Mom, vaccination is a touchy subject. People have extreme opinions about it. You "get to" muddle through all of it to find your happy place.

16) If our baby is a boy, we request circumcision before we leave the hospital.

It is standard to have the boy circumcised, in the hospital, on the third day. However, some cultures wait 8 days for religious reasons. Others don't have it done at all. It was important for me to make it part of my Birth Plan so the nursing staff was aware of our wishes on paper. There was so much hustle and bustle with staff, trying to learn to breastfeed, juggling photos, and welcoming visitors. I did not want to leave the hospital with him uncircumcised as an "oopsie" in case someone forgot to do it. That is what the Birth Plan is for: laying out all your expectations so nothing is missed before leaving for home.

The hospital was kind enough to give us a list of things for the overnight bag. I followed the list and added my own things too. I must say, I felt good about my bag because I was super prepared. Looking back on it, I am thankful I took all the advice to heart and actually carried it out. I am sure these worksheets and preparation suggestions fall upon deaf ears many times. Perhaps some mothers say, "Yeah, yeah I will get to it...." and then, their water breaks two weeks early and there is a mad dash to get an overnight bag together. I did not want to be in that situation. The way I think of it....I am about to enter this uncharted territory that I have never been in before (giving birth) and I have no idea what to expect. So, why not try to get things that I CAN control in order, so when this life-altering event happens, full of things I CANNOT control, I have less to worry about. Then I can focus on the task at hand (childbirth). That is exactly what I did, and getting the bag ready was no joke. I was in the hospital for 3 days and had my toiletries, changes of clothes, and anything else I needed. As many times as I asked my husband to get his bag ready, he never did. He slept in the same shirt for two nights, until my brother-in-law brought him some fresh clothes. I think he even turned his underwear inside out on the second day for freshness. Ha! (Sorry, Honey, but I still think it's funny.) Maybe on the second kid he will listen to his wife.

9

PREPARATION WAS
THE KEY FOR ME

We went in to our final 3D ultrasound appointment on September 14th and my due date was September 26th. We were going every month to see the progress of the baby, as I was over forty and automatically placed in the "high risk" category. (Forty-one to be exact.) This doctor came highly recommended by my OBGYN and he was the best ultrasound tech in his field. So much so, that if he found anything wrong with the growth of the baby, the pregnancy, or my health, he could recommend how to fix it with preventative measures, diet, vitamins, etc. This was so amazing to me and I was happy to have him in my corner!

I was on the table with my tummy exposed and the nurse put the warm gel on my belly button and then walked out. I asked my husband to take a picture since the gel looked like a Hershey's kiss and looked cute. When I later saw the picture, I looked GINORMOUS! I guess when you are pregnant, you don't even know how big you are until you look outside your body at a picture. Our bodies are truly amazing!

The doctor came in to do the exam and he was a delightful man, straight forward, and matter of fact. He was rubbing my belly with the ultrasound wand and said out loud, "Hmmm." I was holding my husband's hand, as I always did, and we looked at each other. Then the doctor told us what he was "hmm-ing" about. He calmly said, "It looks like you are losing amniotic fluid, and the placenta has stopped working." And very smoothly he says, "It looks like we are going to deliver your baby today." My husband's words, "Wait! What?" And for some odd reason, I was very calm about the whole thing. The doctor continued to explain that the baby was okay, we just needed to start the process. My due date was still two weeks away and if we kept the baby in there until term, it would be dangerous. So it was best the baby came out sooner than later. I was so glad to have this information early, and thankful we had this doctor on our baby team.

So, off we went to the hospital! Thank goodness I had my overnight bag in the car. There was no way I could have predicted this. I must say that during my entire pregnancy, I always wondered where I would be when my water broke. Would my husband be home or at work? Would I ruin the carpet in our living room? I had considered any scenarios, but not the one that actually happened. My advice to you, pregnant women, relax and stop trying to figure it out, because it will be nearly impossible. This is one scenario I never would have predicted. I was just overly grateful we were surrounded by doctors when the ultrasound tech had presented us with the news.

It was kind of comical to watch my husband drive me to the hospital, which was only 3 miles away. He sped through the streets as if he was on a raceway. He wove in and out of cars, changing lanes to make it through the next light faster. He was so nervous and anxious, *I* was calming **him** down. I wasn't even having contractions; I had no pain, and it still felt like a normal day. I asked him to just drive normally but he didn't. Let's just say, we got there fast!

GETTING SETTLED IN THE HOSPITAL

We checked into the hospital and they took me into the delivery room. My husband parked the truck and grabbed my bag. This hospital was quite comfortable. The nurses were very kind and attentive. That is a good sign! As I mentioned earlier, everyone was super nice during our tour of the hospital. I highly recommend this! Since birth is such a "personal" event, it is important to have a great team.

It was about 5:00 pm and they started me on an IV drip of Pitocin. This is a medicine that is supposed to induce labor and start contractions. Going into it, I wanted to be as natural as I could, with no medicine if possible. But since our main focus was to get the baby out NOW, I had to follow doctor's orders. I quickly became more than okay with this. Here is my advice, dear ladies: As perfect as you may have it pictured in your head, allow life to throw off your plan. I am a planner for sure! And I wanted to know exactly how the birthing thing worked. Even though I spoke to countless friends, relatives and even acquaintances, no one could have prepared me for this curveball. Sometimes, you just need to roll with the punches. Know that everything will be okay.

So the IV was a-dripping and the Pitocin was a-flowing. However, it did not seem to work immediately. Thankfully, I brought my tablet, so my husband and I streamed a couple of our favorite shows. We passed the time away... we played hangman, watched movies, and before we knew it, it was midnight. They told me not to eat anything in the off-chance they might do an emergency C-Section, I would need to have an empty stomach. But, I was starving and about to do a very long marathon event. My husband snuck me my favorite trail mix and bits of a granola bar. All in all, it worked out fine. I say, if you are hungry, eat, just keep it small.

They rolled in a cot for my husband to sleep on. And I had the big, huge hospital bed. But, because I was about to give birth, you know, only one of the biggest events of my life, I could not sleep! So I hopped on my phone and paid some bills. Answered some emails and scrolled through my social media accounts. In total, I probably slept about 3 or 4 hours that night while my husband snored soundly in the cot by my side.

Through my window, I watched the sunrise. It was about 4:30 am and the nurse came in to check my dilation. To her surprise, the Pitocin was not working as it should. She started me on a second bag in my IV drip. Apparently, the dosage amounts range on a scale from 1 to 20. I started at 1 and worked my way up the scale. All night they increased mine slowly from 1 to 7. Now they brought me up to 12 over the next two hours, and I still had no contractions. Usually, when a patient is up to 12 on the scale, their water breaks, contractions begin, and they start to dilate. My dilation was much slower than it should have been, so they called a doctor in. At 6:30 am the doctor broke my water to get things moving along. I felt a gush and then the contractions began immediately. But I wasn't feeling scared or frightful. I was actually very calm. I was so thankful for all the training and classes I took to prepare for this, because now the skills started to come into play.

Everyone needs to look at a focal point to maintain concentration. Get ready for the biggest physical event of your life, ladies! Pick an actual object that brings you comfort, or something you like to look at. It can be a picture of a sunset or a photo of a family member. (No glass picture frames, please! You do not want to risk broken glass all over yours and baby's stuff in your hospital bag.) You can bring a cute stuffed animal. Something that fits easily into your overnight bag. I chose a stuffed animal bird since it was portable. It was so adorable, it always made me smile.

My husband was at my side, holding my stuffed animal bird, as my focal point. I started the breathing exercises and they really worked. This was where the knowledge came in. If you did not take your Lamaze classes, you can learn it here. Your partners need to learn this too, so grab your partner to read out loud.

It is so important to stay focused. Face each other and maintain eye contact. You need to concentrate on each other and try to match the other one's breathing.

We are going to do 5 breaths.

1) First breath, inhale......exhale and say HEEEEEE for as long as your exhale takes.

2) Now, second breath, inhale again and exhale to say HEE, HEE. Try to cut your exhale in half so each HEE is equal.

3) On the third breath, inhale.... and say HEE, HEE, HEE so you exhale is 3 equal parts. (Are you seeing the pattern here?)

4) On the fourth breath, inhale and as you exhale, make it 4 HEE, HEE, HEE, HEE so it is 4 equal parts.

5) Now the fifth breath inhale... and make your exhale be 5 HEE, HEE, HEE, HEE, HEE The fifth breath is the hardest since it is tough to punch out 5 HEE's. You need a large lung capacity to make them long. But, if you need to force out 5 quick HEE's, that works too!

Now you should feel nice and relaxed. This is how simple it can be to take your mind off childbirth. Practice these 5 breaths a few times with your partner so you know you are in unison and can focus on each other seamlessly.

You can find a video on my website where I actually breakdown this breathing technique a little further.

https://www.myrockerbeez.com/post/breathing

Now Dads / coaches / partners, read this part only to yourself:

During childbirth, you can do this technique for each contraction and all the way through to birth. But instead of keeping a straight count of exhaling HEE's in order of 1, 2, 3, 4, 5, you can mix it up! Partners, you can hold up one hand and pick any number. Go 3, 1, 5 or whatever order to keep Momma on her toes. Each number would tell her how many HEE's she needs to do on her exhale. That is a good way to keep her mind off of what is happening down there and keep her focused on you. Maintain eye contact all the way and using the focal point. Remember, you are breathing with her as her coach, matching each other's rhythm of breaths along the way.

Take Momma's hand and hold the meaty part between her thumb and first finger. Get ready to squeeze. Guide her through these five breaths as described above (1, 2, 3, 4, and 5) and slightly squeeze the meat of her hand. As each breath continues, squeeze harder and harder, increasing gradually. By the time you reach the fifth breath, you should be squeezing the hardest you can. It will amaze you at how she will barely feel this because of the breathing! Once the five breaths finish, you can relax and take a break, release the hand and see how she feels. Now the fun begins!

Okay, Momma, ask your partner / coach to show you just how hard they were squeezing your hand by the fifth breath. You won't believe it! It was SO hard! Mine honestly hurt so bad, I had to tell my husband to stop. He could not even show me his full strength. That is the amazing power of this type of breathing and focus. While I was doing the breathing exercises, I did not feel it! This is exactly the way I got through my entire childbirth without feeling any pain.

Why does this work? Muscles need oxygen to function and relax so if you hold your breath and deny them oxygen, you will have pain. If you can be free flowing and allow oxygen to flow in and out to all your cells and muscles, you will alleviate any cramping or pain. As I had contractions and continued my breathing, I did not have any pain! I was "uncomfortable" yes, but I did not have pain. It just felt different.

Unfortunately, too many women have such pain during childbirth. Or young, pregnant moms-to-be, hear such horror stories from their moms or aunts of what they went through. However, it doesn't have to be that way. I want to teach you how to find your calm, how to breathe, and how to let your partner be your strength. Making you stronger together; to be there for the baby to come into this world. There will be a long road to recovery, but you can bask in the glow of beauty, not grovel in fear and unknown.

I had a peaceful, beautiful childbirth! I did it. My mom spoke of this and I did not know it was possible until I experienced it myself. I did **NOT** feel the birth, I swear to you; I did not feel any pain at all! It was beautiful and smooth and I owe it all to the breathing exercises. I know I am not the first and certainly not the last, but I want you to know that it CAN be done! What am I talking about? I mean the actual birth, the ring of fire, as your baby is coming through the birth canal, crowning, the head coming out and the rest of the baby. Well, as funny as it may sound, I didn't feel pain. Yes, you read it right. I did NOT feel pain as the baby came out! Honest to God truth, hand sworn to the heavens. My husband can attest to it (he was there), as well as the doctor and the many nurses. How did I do it? With lots of focus and the breathing exercises I just shared with you. My experience of being all natural, no pain relieving drugs, just me, the baby, and my husband! Believe it or not, my hubby was a key component in all of this. I could not have done it without him!

This may sound a little awkward, but bear with me. Once I learned this breathing technique, I still had about two more months of pregnancy. I would try to practice this breathing daily. Every time I had a bowel movement, I would breathe and keep oxygen flowing to the muscles. Not that I would do all 5 breaths every time, but I would focus on my breathing while going to the bathroom. Sometimes when you are pregnant, it is hard to have a bowel movement, and many women get constipated. I figured out that if you push, take a deep inhale while pausing that push (not releasing it), then exhale and push again, this is a very close mimic to pushing for childbirth. By practicing this on a daily basis, it became second nature to me, and I was never constipated!

10

IT'S SHOWTIME!

Back to the birth: The nurse kept asking me if I wanted the epidural, because once you get past a certain threshold, they are not able to give it to you anymore. I kept telling her NO, I did not want it and to please stop asking me. She didn't, she kept asking all the way up until the last possible moment. I guess it is so rare that people deny it, she wanted to make sure.

Contractions started to get closer together and I felt like an immediate push. I called the nurse to tell her it was time! She did not think I had been in labor long enough for it to be time. So she reached down to check my dilation and I was at 8 cm. That is huge! When you get to 10 cm you are ready to give birth. (Just to put this in perspective, 10 cm is about the size of a rice cake. Yes, it gets that big!) The nurse was surprised I had progressed so far so fast and had me move onto the delivery table. Feet in the stirrups, and I was ready to go. But... oh no, my doctor was in surgery! They were telling me not to push and I was trying my best to hold my baby in. It's like rushing to the bathroom for a bowel movement when it is right on the edge and you sit on the toilet and you have to hold it. It was a very hard thing to do, but I kept breathing. Still, I had 2 cm more to dilate. It seemed like an eternity, and then the doctor finally came in, dressed in full gear.

The delivery room was full. There were about 6 or 8 nurses plus my doctor. I pushed and maintained my breathing. The entire time my husband was right by my side, guiding me through the breathing. He was on my left, holding my left foot in one hand and my left hand in the other. A nurse was on my right, holding my right foot and gripping my right hand. I felt like I was bracing myself for a rocket ship take-off. My baby's head was emerging and all the nurses encouraged me to keep on pushing. I was very aware of my surroundings and noticed everything I was feeling. It wasn't much. My husband maintained good eye contact with me and was a strong guide as we did the breathing exercises together. Now, I am not sure if the breathing helped take my mind off what was happening "down there" or if it was actually science taking over and sending tons of oxygen to the areas in need. All I know is, it just worked. Possibly, a combination of both. Regardless, getting the head through the birth canal was the hardest part of this entire process.

I finally dilated to 10 cm, but my baby's head felt too big, like it wouldn't fit. The doctor said, "I know it hurts, the ring of fire, but give me one big push!" (Ring of fire is a hot sensation like your vagina is burning at the very moment your baby's head starts crowning.) I sat up and said, "I don't feel a ring of fire and it doesn't hurt at all. What should I do?" I thought I was doing it wrong this whole time. All the nurses looked up at me, jaws dropped, looked at each other, and in the perfect unison yelled, "Then PUSH!" I felt like I was in a movie! I pushed as hard as I could and still could not get my baby's head through. No, it was not going to fit. The doctor informed me she would like to perform an episiotomy. (This is where they make a small incision on the side of my vaginal wall to allow the baby to pass.) Yes, of course, lady! "Do whatever you have to do!" I said. She gave me a local numbing agent, a little slit, and out came my baby's head!

The worst was over, yet I still had to pass the rest of my baby. There was more pushing, breathing, focusing, and I soon felt the thump, thump of the shoulders, then boom, boom of the legs as they came out. It was a strange sensation, but astounding at the same time. Like, "Hey, I am making a person right now." Mind blowing, at best! It's a boy! Now the umbilical cord is still attached remember? So there was that. We asked for "delayed cord cutting" since the placenta was still alive inside of me and blood was still flowing to our baby. For an extra 4-8 minutes, our son received that excellent placental blood. Remember, if you cut the cord early, your baby loses out on all those nutrients. We wanted to keep it longer, and they respected our wishes on this. (Part of the Birth Plan).

Next, I had to pass the placenta which was small potatoes compared to what I just went through. I breathed a little more, pushed a little more, calmed down from the storm while they cleaned my baby. It seemed like an hour but was only a few minutes, until I finally got to hold my son. It was such a beautiful moment! My husband did a fist pump to the sky like, "Yeah! It's a boy!" He hugged us both so tight and we sobbed in each other's arms. We worked so hard for this moment! Here we were, just us three. Everything and everyone around us just melted away for a few moments. We waited nine months to meet our son, and now he was finally here in our arms. What a feeling, it was indescribable!

The nurse came over and interrupted our moment, but simply because I needed to start feeding him right away. She positioned him so he could latch onto my breast and he took a few sips then fell asleep. Of course, he was tired from the traumatic journey he just travelled. And that's ok, because so was I. They took my little bundle and put him in his teeny tiny cradle. It was all clear acrylic so I could see a full view of him from any angle. What a handsome guy!

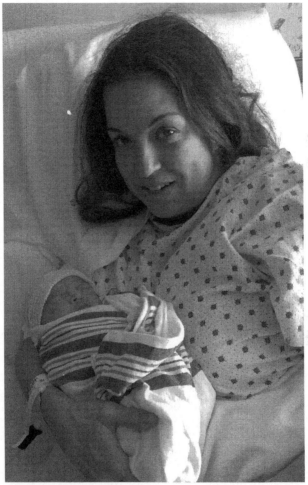

Photo by Peter Famiglietti

SOAKING IT ALL IN

For about an hour, my husband and I just talked and felt so elated, the ultimate joy that every parent feels on that special day. We were that rare couple that did not find out the sex of the baby until this day. Yes, we received a lot of grey and yellow baby clothes, but it didn't matter. This day and age of gender reveal parties and learning the sex early on, for me, it would have taken something special away from this moment. Only my husband and I knew what we had right when it happened because we were there, and it was sacred. I would never trade that moment in for a pink or blue reveal cake or balloon bouquet. But that was just me. If I have another baby, I would do it again in a heartbeat. Keeping the gender a surprise until the baby is born, made the day all that more exciting. It was like the cherry on top of an already super amazing hot fudge sundae. I highly recommend it for all.

Now the doctor had to get in there and clean me up She stitched the incision, and made sure all of the placenta had exited gracefully. And it did. The enormous ball in my stomach had gone down and I felt weird, after having been a basketball for the past month. My husband and I were over the moon, just staring at our little guy and at each other with huge smiles. We could not believe he was finally here. One of the nurses looked over to us and said, "Aren't you going to call anybody?" Oh yeah! We had family members on pins and needles as they waited to hear the outcome. It was over an hour since our little one arrived and we were just basking in every moment.

The very first call we made was across the country to my in-laws. We named our son after my husband's father, as this is an Italian tradition. Upon hearing this news, proud Grandpa got all choked up and felt so honored and equally surprised. I love surprises and sharing, "It's a boy!" with everyone. Saying his name for the first time, made me smile even more on this joyous day. We called my mom next. She lived locally and wanted to see the baby right away. I asked her to bring me some In-&-Out Burger. If you're from California, you know what I am talking about. Mind you, I had not eaten for the past twenty-four hours except for a few small bites of some nuts and seeds. I needed a hefty meal after I just pushed a watermelon through a doughnut hole. I was starving! And here came a craving, I guess. I can still remember my order: a hamburger, French fries, and a vanilla shake. This may not have been the healthiest of choices, but it was fast, better than hospital food, and someone was bringing it to me. My labor was considered short, by hospital industry standards. The doctor broke my water around 6:30 am and I gave birth by 2:36 pm. Only 8 hours was pretty good. Still, I was famished!

Mom and her boyfriend came with food in hand. He's a photographer and offered to take pictures of us. I wasn't sure that I even wanted any pictures so soon. But I'm so glad I'd said yes! He took some great shots of us and our brand new baby. I highly recommend having someone take pictures right after the delivery. We still cherish every single one, as they are very special to us. Our hospital even offered a service where a photographer came in the day after he was born to do a photo shoot. If you have this opportunity, **do it!** It was a little bit expensive, but worth every penny! These were such precious moments, and we have blown up pictures of him on our walls today. My boy, one day old. I will never get that again. So wonderful!

We stayed in the delivery room for a few hours while they took footprints of our little guy. My husband made sure to follow him everywhere in the hospital. Make sure you do this! You do not want the hospital staff to do "routine" things to a newborn that you may not have wanted done at all.

We had learned from my sister's experience, so I made sure my husband followed the staff around like a hawk to keep our baby free from unnecessary medications. He asked a lot of questions, and made sure they explained every procedure to him *before* they did it. Our baby got a few shots, which we knew were coming, got a belly button clamp (and my hubby got to cut the cord!), and he was scheduled for his circumcision, which would happen in a day or two.

They finally moved us over to a recovery room. It was maybe four hours after I had given birth and I wanted to get up and stretch my legs. My room was just down the hall a bit, so a nurse guided me to it. As I passed the nurses' station, about five nurses were staring at me with their mouths wide open. One nurse even said to me, "You're walking? How are you walking right now? Didn't you just give birth?" I guess it is not typical for Mommas to walk after giving birth for multiple reasons: exhaustion, having an epidural, weakness, a long labor, or complications. I considered myself lucky that I was feeling good enough to walk after giving birth.

This hospital was really nice because I had my own private room. I have heard of hospitals jamming new moms together where they need to share a room and the only thing between them was a curtain. This hospital and staff took much better care of new moms and their babies. I had my own bathroom and a door that closed and locked. I even had my own visitor's room off to the side where people could hold my baby and visit with my husband if I was sleeping. This came in handy since they like to keep you in the hospital for three days. The next few days were filled with visitors.

11

MY BREASTFEEDING TIPS THAT WORKED

Breastfeeding did not come easy for me. It was a little weird, and it took me a while to get the hang of it. The hospital gave me a set of two nipple shields,* which are a **must have** in the beginning. If you have never heard of these, get them! They are small silicone nipples, with a flat piece that lays against your breast, almost like a suction cup, but it just stays there on its own. It allows the milk to flow through tiny holes and the baby can take it all the way into their mouth.

*Take a look at my Resource Page at the back of this book to order yours (page 219)

Since my nipple did not reach that far, this acted as an extension. ***It saved my ability to breast feed***!

Right here is where I think a lot of women stop breastfeeding. It becomes physically difficult, painful, or they cannot get a good latch. Perhaps not every hospital provides nipple shields as an option. This is why I want you to know about it here. Get them on your own. If your hospital gives them out for free, bonus! You will have 2 sets. Breastfeeding it THE MOST IMPORTANT THING you can do for your baby. It is the best, so fight hard, my dear Mommas, to do it any way you can!

When my mom saw them, she said, "WOW! I wish they had these when I had you girls." As the story goes, I bit her nipple so hard, she fainted from the pain. If she had a nipple shield it would have helped her feel it less. The lactation consultant told me my nipples were "not protruded enough" which caused me to have a poor latch. The nipple shields would help my baby latch on in my situation. Some women have inverted nipples where they actually cave in. Other women may have flat nipples which give the baby little to latch onto. Mine were there, but they weren't big enough for my baby to get enough to grab onto to drink. Who knew there were so many variations of nipples? I certainly learned a lot here.

The main job of a nipple shield is to encourage your nipple to stretch to where it needs to be stretched to, in order for your baby to have a full latch. This means your baby has a mouth full of nipple, areola, and breast tissue to create enough suction to draw milk. When a mother reaches this point, she has mastered the art of breastfeeding and her baby can latch and drink seamlessly. Whelp, I never really mastered it. My nipple did not stretch to where it needed to be, so I kept using my shields for about six months. And honestly, I could not seem to find a latch without them, as it was much more comfortable. If you think about how much skin / nipple a baby needs to grab onto, it's kind of a lot. With breastfeeding can also come some nasty breast chaffing, dryness, bleeding, and chapping on your nipple, which many women experience. Yet, they still needed to breastfeed their baby through all of this, trying different breast creams, ice cubes, whatever works. OR, use a nipple shield and skip all of this! Hello? It was a simple choice for me. The only downside was, carrying them with me, literally everywhere I went and keeping them clean. But, I had a little pack full of nipple shields, nursing cups (more in a minute on this), bottle bags, and a vile with a lid for extra milk. A "nursing kit," if you will, for me and my baby to take everywhere. When I got home, I washed and sterilized it all, and schooled my husband on how to do it so I could take a rest sometimes too.

Now, what is a nursing cup you ask? Well, this was something they **did** have way back when my mother was breastfeeding, and my mom actually introduced me to these. In fact, she had the originals saved, as they stood the test of time, she gifted them to me one day. But something about using such a personal item made me feel weird, so I graciously accepted the gift, then bought my own set. Still, what are they? Nursing cups* are milk catchers! Shaped like half of a baseball, but hollow. The flat side has a hole in it for your nipple. It sits right inside your nursing bra and catches the milk as it drips out while breastfeeding on the other side. Whenever a baby nurses, that stimulates both breasts to produce milk. It is important to catch this milk so you can build up a backup supply in your freezer. Try to always have plenty for when you might travel with your baby, to make baby food, or to give your partner a chance to bottle feed sometimes.

Most likely every woman has experienced breastfeeding the baby on one boob and leaking milk out of the other boob that is not in use. And, you have probably heard people refer to breast milk as "liquid gold." Please never waste one drop! Traditionally, women have used "*nursing pads*" which can be disposable or washable. Since lots of Mommas want to "Go Green" they have chosen the washable and reusable type. Nursing pads look like flat round pancakes made out of terry cloth that catch excess milk, and can be thrown into the wash. But it still does not address the fact that the breast milk is now in the washing machine, not the baby or the freezer! Of course, we need *something* to keep our shirts from getting wet. But why not choose a device that can capture milk for later?

I belonged to a nursing group and no one had ever seen nursing cups before, not even the instructor. So I felt so inclined to share this info with other Mommas. I can't believe they are not more widespread than this. I share this info so more people can be aware of them. There is only one chance in your life to breastfeed your precious baby you carried for nine months. Make every drop counts! Help your baby get the most out of this "liquid gold" so they can have the strongest bones, smartest brain, healthiest organs, best hair, skin, and good digestion. There is only one chance! Don't use nursing pads and waste a drop. Catch it all so they can drink it all!

*Get your nursing cups on my website too! Be sure to check the Resource Page 219 at the end of this book. I have organized everything all in one place for you, Momma. ☺

WHERE THERE IS MILK, THERE WILL BE POOP!

When the baby eats a lot of volume, expect the same amount of volume on the backend, if you know what I mean. Meconium is the first poop of life, and THANK GOD my mom was there to help me. This was no regular poop like you or I might have, but it was not diarrhea either. It was worse, way worse, so prepare yourself, as no one really prepared me! It is very clear when a baby makes their first poop of life since they are pushing, struggling, and maybe even crying a little bit. Their little body has been in amniotic fluid for nine months, so they probably don't even understand what the heck is happening here. My little guy was grunting and squinting, his face turned bright red like a tomato. Mom said, "Oh, he is pooping! Can I change his first poop for you?" Why, of course, my dear, Momma, go for it! Thank goodness because I did not know what she was in for. But having 3 grown kids, and now her 5th grandchild, she was a pro! When she opened up his diaper, it was black, like the color of my laptop. Like asphalt even. And the consistency was very sticky, worse than bubble gum or peanut butter. As if you mixed honey, glue and sawdust. It stuck all over his bottom and on some of his family jewels too. But there went Mom, like a champ, she dug in there with baby wipes and her mad skills. She taught me a valuable tip that made the next diaper change a breeze.

After you get the baby all cleaned up, take some diaper cream and rub it all over his anus and surrounding cheek area. That way, when the next meconium makes its debut, it will be an easy cleanup. It works really well since this stuff is incredibly sticky! You can expect to have 5-7 of these bowel movements until things get regulated and eating gets on a good schedule. This is the transition from feeding baby through the umbilical cord to feeding through the mouth. What amazing miracles we hold in our arms here. Science is awesome!

12

TAKING MY BABY HOME

They had to wheel me out in a wheelchair, even though I could walk perfectly fine. Just a precaution, I guess. My husband went to get the truck while I brought our baby out. It was a little tricky to get him into the car seat. Since we were first-timers and everything, it was nerve-wracking handling our precious cargo who was so delicate. We had to put his teeny, tiny arms through the shoulder straps. And buckle around his lap and legs. Not only are the straps so huge, we were worried we might make it too tight. But he was safe, secure, and probably slept the entire way home. We could not see him since he was facing the backseat for safety. I had never seen my husband drive so slow before in my life!

Walking in the door with him was so surreal. Very life changing and it hit me like a ton of bricks, but in a good way! From this point forward, we were three. There was a new little life as part of our family. We have a son! What an amazing thing that we left our home with me pregnant, and three days later he was here in my arms. I just felt so proud in that moment.

In our birthing class they did address how to handle bringing home a baby when you have a pet. We have a small Chihuahua mix who I have had for ten years. Now we were bringing a little baby into her home that will cry, wake her up at night, and make strange sounds she has never heard before. The best way to introduce our son was for my husband and me to greet our dog first. I picked her up, hugged her, and let her know that I loved her just the same. Then I slowly introduced my son to her. I gave our dog a blanket that my son had been wrapped in over the past few days, and put it in her dog bed. This lets the pup know the baby's scent, it felt safe in her bed, and helped her understand this new little being was going to be a friend.

One key point is to never let the dog be higher than the baby. If a dog is used to being on the sofa, which our dog was, and the baby is on the floor, the dog has all the power. Do not let the dog be in a power positon over the baby, otherwise the pet will think they are in charge. You do not want this! Sorry puppy, you cannot come on the couch anymore. It took a little bit of training for our dog to live a little differently than she was used to. But after a few days, she was lying next to the crib while my son slept, as if she were protecting her new friend. Once she saw how precious this new gift was to us, she understood this tiny guy was something special and someone to watch over. It was cute.

The Pack-n-Play came in handy with our two-story home. He had his sleeping place in our room in a bassinet upstairs for night times, but we wanted another sleeping area downstairs for naps. That way, we could keep a close eye on him, have him get used to our everyday noises, and be able to fall asleep like a champ! This was a wonderful way to teach our baby when it was time to sleep, it didn't matter what was going on around him (TV, music, doing the dishes, etc....). He could pretty much sleep through anything.

We put up a clothing caddy in the living room downstairs and had his dresser fully stocked with clothes in his bedroom upstairs. It is an excellent idea to have fresh onesies, pants, shirts, and socks close by wherever you are feeding, napping or changing your baby. There will be plenty of spit ups, milk drips, pee overflows, and poop explosions. I also had a nursing station downstairs on the sofa and upstairs in my bedroom. Try to have duplicates of everything. If you have a two-story home, then two of everything. If you have a single-story home, consider yourself lucky to not have to deal with stairs. But you could still have multiple changing stations in different areas. It will make your life way more efficient to have all these stations nearby and ready.

In the beginning, it is key to have two separate areas for sleeping and changing diapers. Since new parents are amateurs (we certainly were) I would venture to say at least 50% of the time, a spill would get onto the changing area. ***Try not to ever change the baby where he sleeps.*** Otherwise, you will have more laundry to do and it will take longer to put your baby to sleep as you are trying to clean up messy bedding in the middle of the night. If the changing table gets ruined, no big deal. Your baby's bed will still be clean and dry so you can put him back to sleep quickly after a diaper change. You can always deal with the changing table later if you need to.

One time, my husband was changing our boy in the parking lot of a restaurant. It was one of our earliest outings with a newborn. We were both dressed up nicely and I specifically remember he had on a white polo shirt and some light khaki shorts. He looked so handsome. He parked, and brought our son up to the driver's seat of his truck. The truck was nice and high so changing a baby was easier than changing him in my low, four-door compact car. As soon as he opened the diaper to change him, our baby boy lifted his legs and made the biggest projectile diarrhea I had ever seen! It shot out with the force of a drinking fountain and the same amount of height. I didn't know this was humanly possible! Thank God for my husband's ninja-like reflexes! He dodged this poo fountain and saved his white shirt and khaki shorts from being destroyed. I cannot say the same for the parking lot though! To this day, we still laugh about it.

The point of this story was to emphasize that opening up a newborn diaper could be like a volcano, a geyser, or any other force of nature. Anything and everything is possible. You will become an expert on smells, colors, and textures. You will have conversations with your partner about how it was, if he had a blowout, needed a new change of clothes, or got it all over the changing area. Prepare yourself! This is an area of expertise you never thought you would have in your knowledge bank!

Now that you know diaper duty is a messy situation, this was where all my diaper caddies became useful. We had a diaper caddy for the downstairs, a station to change in his room upstairs, and another one in our room for middle of the night changes. No one wants to carry a dripping wet, cranky, squirmy baby from downstairs all the way upstairs simply because that is where his room is. Make your life easier by doing this. Trust me, you will appreciate the convenience.

Here is a HUGE TIP I didn't figure out until about one year in. Wherever you have the baby's cushy, pillow-top diaper changing table, put a small blanket on top of whatever cute fitted sheet you have over it. It will make a world of difference. Even though I had two of everything (sheets, changing covers, and diaper pad covers) everything would still get ruined and I needed to constantly rotate, which meant more laundry, more often. Save yourself some time and register for 12-20 burping, swaddle, and baby blankets. That way, if the baby leaks onto the diaper changing table, you just swap out the blanket and not the entire sheet set.

Getting into the groove of things took a little while. It took me about a week before I stepped foot outside the house. My husband made me and my son a little morning surprise breakfast outside on our beautiful California patio. Of course, the sun was shining and the weather was absolutely beautiful! He cut up some delicious fruit and cheese, poured orange juice, buttered toast, and made some much needed coffee! It was perfect. I felt the sun on my face for the first time after a week and breathed in fresh air. It was amazing. My baby was in his cuddle cove next to me with his hood up for a little shade while he napped. I don't think he even knew what was going on, but it was perfect! For the first time, I started to feel like myself again.

Photo by Peter Famiglietti

There is a big difference between having a full-time staff of nurses at the hospital and then getting home and having to do everything by yourself. Once you walk into your home, with a new baby in your arms, YOU are the one the baby will need for the next year or more! You have the milk, you have the mother's touch, and only you have the soothing voice this baby has heard for the past nine months. Therefore, the first week was a whirlwind. I was in a cloud of fog trying to find my rhythm and my baby's too. Taking care of my baby feels like the number one priority, but taking care of yourself, **should** be number one. Replenishing your food makes more milk. Healing your undercarriage gives you the ability to move around a whole lot better. Sleep is necessary for both of you. As hard as it sounds to put yourself first, you need to at least try. I wish I knew ahead of time, what I am about to tell you in the next chapter. I just had to figure it out for myself. Had I known, I would have put myself first a lot more.

13

WHAT I WISH I KNEW
BEFORE I WAS IN IT

The hospital sent me home with my own little kit to care for my aching vagina. ☹ Yeah, childbirth is a lot and it took me about 6 weeks to recover completely. Do not be put off by this, as every woman who birthed vaginally, goes through this. But it doesn't matter. You hold the greatest gift in your arms and it is worth every ache and pain. I write this chapter to let you know what to expect, not to scare you into never wanting to have a baby. I wish I knew *all* of this beforehand, then mentally, I would have been more prepared. So here you go!

After my baby was born, I had to take care of myself using the "three-step process" the nurses taught me in the hospital, every time I went to the bathroom. This was so important to follow, so your body heals quickly and without infection. Your biscuit already feels like somebody kicked it with a steel-toed boot. In my case, I had stitches, so not only the boot kick, but a rip, like a hole in my jeans, but down there. Yeah, it hurt. Make sure to follow the protocol and it will help to ease your pain.

Step1: After I peed or pooped, I remained seated on the toilet, and took this squishy plastic bottle that had a spout on it, kind of like a squirter. I filled it with warm water and squirted my entire undercarriage from front to back with the water. Not only did it feel good, it flushed everything out to keep any infection from forming. Honestly, it is like having an open wound down there and it is important to take care of it and change "the dressings" often.

Step 2: I lined my big granny underwear with huge maxi pads they sent me home with from the hospital. I have never seen a maxi this big in my life! It looked like a surfboard or possibly a kayak. Anyway, they worked great because I continued to bleed for about a week. It is totally normal, just something I didn't expect.

On a side note: You may want to purchase these yacht size maxi pads about a month before your due date. That way, when your water breaks, you can be ready to put one on as you ride in the car to the hospital. You won't have to worry about leaking amniotic fluid or blood all over your clothes and car.

Step 3: I sprayed my entire bottom with cooling spray. This was an aerosol can of cooling goodness that put an icy layer on my skin to relax and soothe everything. This was key, otherwise it would have been painful and burning all the time. I also used Tucks medicated pads with witch-hazel. These soothed very nicely too. You can just line your maxi pad with these and pull up your underwear.

After these three steps my biscuit felt soothed and relaxed. On the second day home, I felt adventurous and wanted to see what all the fuss was about. So I took a look at everything going on down there. I had not seen it since I gave birth. I took a hand mirror so I could see and it wasn't pretty. From the front of my vulva, past my butthole, and above was a dark purple, brown, and almost black in some areas! It was so dark and everything was numb. I couldn't tell if it was a bruise or diarrhea smeared everywhere across my stuff! I just had a bowel movement, and I thought I wiped pretty well, but I honestly did not even know what was happening. Oh and by the way, bowel movements tend to be soft for a few days and it will hurt to wipe. You may even get a couple of hemorrhoids from all the pushing during childbirth. So you just kind of dab, dab, dab as best you can and hope you got it all. The brown and black color everywhere really freaked me out! I called my husband, while I was still in the bathroom, to come look and help me figure out what the heck was going on. Was this poo or was it permanently on my skin?

Me: *"Babe! Can you come in here please?"*

Him: *"Are you ok?"*

Me: *"I don't know. This is going to be gross but I need some help."*

Him: *"OK."*

My gracious husband, ready for any situation. God love him!

Me: *"Can you please look, try not to freak out, and tell me if this is poo or a bruise?"*

Him: *"Sure." Pause for the investigation..... "It's a bruise."*

Me: *"For reals?"*

Him: *"Yes, it is a huge bruise. I mean, think of what you just went through, Honey. Of course it will be bruised."*

(How does he even know this? Oh yeah, he saw the birth happen live. Okay, I believe him.)

Me: *"Thanks babe. I love you!"*

Him: *"Love you too!"*

The biggest bruise I have ever had in my life! I guess since everything gets stretched, pushed, and torn down there it bruises. Big time!

Okay, now I got that part figured out, I sent him out of the bathroom and continued to investigate. Every time I went to the bathroom and wiped with my dab, dab, dabs, I felt this weird bump. I wanted to see what it was. I took my trusty hand mirror and tried to contort so I could see it. What I saw was really strange, as I had never seen anything like it before. It was round, shiny, and red. It looked like a cherry tomato, hanging out of my vagina! What was this? I was too embarrassed to ask my husband to come back and look again, so I just kept it to myself. After a few phone calls to the nurse line and my doctor's office, I learned that sometimes women push so hard, part of their uterus can stretch and come out, referred to as uterine prolapse. Huh? This was a thing? Yes, a thing that I was sporting right about now. Great! Just add it to the list of problems. It was shiny, bloody, and when I touched it, there was no feeling because there are no nerve endings on it. Of course, it doesn't, it is an internal organ people! It was the strangest thing. It didn't hurt, it was just there. How the heck was I supposed to get this red ball back in there? A few times I tried to push it in with my finger. It didn't work. I googled, researched, and found out Kegel exercises could fix all. Your uterus shrinks back to how it was before childbirth. It just takes time. Like, a long time! In my case, it took about six weeks to get it back in. But rest assured, it went back in, and it stayed there! This does not happen to everybody, and I hope it doesn't happen to you. However, had I known about this ahead of time as even a remote possibility, I would have done my Kegel exercises long before this day!

With all this bleeding, bruising, burning, and now hanging, I felt so sore from my belly button to my knees. Muscles were sore, bones had shifted, and it hurt to walk. It was also incredibly difficult to go up and down the stairs of our two-story condo. My husband, graciously blew up the inflatable mattress and made a bed for both of us downstairs on the first level. The key to recovery is to sleep, and people will tell you again and again, to sleep when the baby sleeps. Thankfully, now I had a place to rest my head on the first floor. My goal was to only go up the stairs once a day to shower and go to our real bed at night in our master bedroom. But, I needed to lean on my husband to get there. Every night we hobbled up the stairs together. For better or for worse, right? Thank God for my man! I love my husband so much!

And the other part of my vagina care kit included a plastic bed pan looking device. I set this on the inside of the toilet bowl rim, filled it with warm water, and sat in it. I did this every night before my shower. It was like a soothing yoga class for my aching parts. Ohm! Then I would take a shower, let more water run and soothe everything. Then bed!

While you are in the mode of taking care of yourself, two more things that helped me so much were cocoa butter and a corset.* My sister gave me all her corsets she used after birthing three children and she said it was key to keeping her figure. Hey, what did I have to lose, except the baby weight! I followed the steps and I am proud to say, I had no stretch marks whatsoever and even got my waist back. Every night after the shower, I lathered my entire body with cocoa butter with special focus on my tummy, lower back, butt and thighs. These are the main areas where women tend to get stretch marks. Then I would put on the corset and go to sleep. I also lathered myself with

*Get your corset and cocoa butter on my Resource Page 219

cocoa butter since the day I found out I was pregnant. With my growing belly, it helped moisturize the skin so much it did not have a chance to dry out or get stretch marks.

The corset helped put everything back into place after giving birth: vital organs, abdominal muscles, and my hips. I slept with it because it was a little uncomfortable. I did not want to wear it 24/7 but at least half of the day. I would take it on and off. I probably wore it a total of 12 hours in a 24-hour period. Since all my muscles got so stretched and overworked, they needed a little help to get back to normal. It worked! Once I felt I could pull myself out of bed using my abs again instead of my arms, or just rolling out of bed, I stopped wearing it. I'd say it was about six months after giving birth.

I have heard of women getting loose skin flab or things just "not bouncing back." Everyone is different, but this worked for me. If I have a way to help prevent something, I will share it. Perhaps those women didn't know what to do and if they had, it may have helped. Perhaps some women are prone to loose skin and stretch marks because their mothers had them, and all their mothers before her in the family line. I am not a scientist, and can't explain why cells respond the way they do in some and not in others. But some key factors to skin elasticity are hydration, not only topical, like lotion but also internal, like drinking tons of water. I did both! Every cell in your body needs water to survive and be able to work to its full potential. If a cell is not fully hydrated, it will be weak. Try it out and if it works, it works!

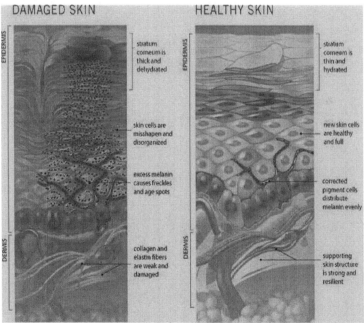

Photo courtesy of www.shutterstock.com

14

GETTING MY BABY TO SLEEP, AND SLEEP WELL

It took about 3 days to figure out the rhythm of my baby's eating, sleeping and pooping schedule. But we made sure our house was set up to make it all happen, as listed in the checklists. I found five key components I always made sure to have in place whenever it was nap time or bedtime:

1) **Sound Machine**
2) **Swaddle**
3) **Pacifier**
4) **Dark Room**
5) **Fill Baby's Tummy**

Since we decided against having a newborn in the bed with us, he slept in the bassinet next to our bed. The first few nights I had very little sleep. Every peep he made I sat up thinking he needed to be changed, fed or something. It was rough since we had not figured out our rhythm for feeding-times, diaper changes, etc.... So on day 3 we introduced the sound machine. YEAH! An absolute lifesaver!

Ours had several modes, beach waves, heartbeat, birds, river, and rain. We chose beach waves as it seemed like the most soothing sound for all three of us. It helped me sleep because it would drown out the little coos and teeny tiny groans he would make throughout the night. Those were about every five minutes and I would wake up frantically for each and every one of them. The sound machine allowed me to sleep soundly, but not too soundly. I could still hear his cries for feeding time.

When a baby sleeps through the night, it is a beautiful thing for us parents. While I was pregnant, I did a ton of research and interviewed many Mommas to find out what worked. Our baby started sleeping through the night at four months old and has been ever since. Though every baby is different, try these tips that worked for us.

1. Sound Machine: Find one that plays ocean or nature sounds. It does something magical for the baby. It gives them a sense of security. All babies wake up during the night a few times, and the soothing sound lets them know it is still sleeping time. They can open their eyes, see the dark room and hear the sounds. Then, they lightly drift back to sleep without a fuss.

2. Swaddle: Get a good swaddle cloth with a little stretch to the fabric. Swaddling is a great way to give your newborn the feeling of being in the womb again. My husband is an expert swaddler. He spent many nights on YouTube researching the best swaddle to use. Since my son is strong and mighty, he could break out of most swaddle styles. Until we found the one that worked. We called it baby burrito, because he literally looked like a burrito by the time my husband was done with him. Keep trying different ones until you find the one that works for your little bundle.

3. Pacifier: We chose to use one, after much research, since it was more orthodontically correct for his teeth and growing jaw than thumb sucking. I could also wean him off of it and later remove the pacifier, but you can't remove a thumb! We found it to be a great comfort for him at night, unless it fell out, of course! If you choose to go with a pacifier, there is a learning curve on keeping it in the baby's mouth. Be prepared for this. My baby did very well most nights. And once he understood how uncomfortable he was without it, he learned to keep it in on his own. Putting it back in for your baby will most likely fall on you, dear Momma. You will have the trained ear to listen for anything and everything your baby needs throughout the night, while your partner sleeps soundly through it all. But there is light at the end of this tunnel. Once he was able to sit up and roll over, on his own, he would magically find his pacifier and put it back in by himself.

4. Dark Room: Black out curtains help with blocking all the light from the windows. We have these curtains on our master bedroom windows. So when our son slept on our room, it was very dark. We made sure to install a set in his nursery too. That way, when he was ready to go into his own room, things would stay consistent. Everything we did was to try and mimic the womb. Darkness was all he knew for nine months. This brought him much comfort. Some parents think babies need a night light so they won't be scared. Perhaps it is more for the parents than the baby. Try darkness or a night light, as every baby is different. But my boy sure loved the darkness and still does.

5. Fill Baby's Tummy: Babies sleep best on a full stomach. If they go to bed hungry, they will be awake shortly after, crying for a midnight snack. Since I breastfed, exclusively, my husband wanted a chance to have some bonding time with our baby too. He fed our son a big bottle of breastmilk every night before bed as his last meal. This worked extremely well for all of us. It gave me a break from actual breastfeeding, and while they were bonding, I pumped every night alongside them. That pumped milk then became the bottle of milk for the following night. And sometimes during pumping, I would get more than one full bottle. I was an over-producer, so this setup allowed me to slowly build a milk stash in the freezer on a daily basis. This was a win-win all the way around. Putting the baby to bed on a full stomach is super important to having him sleep through the night. Win! My husband spent quality time with our son and bonded with him. Double win! And my boy got to fall right to sleep in

Daddy's arms. Triple win! It was beautiful and a very good plan for all of us.

The best bottle system I ever found didn't involve a bottle at all! Weird, I know, but stay with me here. It involved milk bags, a screw top nipple attachment, and a bottle holder. It is the Kiinde bottle system.* I chose this one because it saved me so much time from washing bottles, transferring milk, or even heating it up. The way it worked was incredibly easy for me, a Momma on the go. Instead of pouring your freshly pumped breast milk into a hard plastic or glass bottle, I pumped it directly into the Kiinde plastic milk bag. Then I easily screwed on the top, and the milk went right into my refrigerator or freezer. When my husband was ready to do his bedtime feeding, he would take the bag from the fridge, and warm it up between his hands. Like Mr. Miagi style! (Karate Kid reference if you are old enough to understand it. LOL!) This was amazing for anytime or anywhere! With traditional bottles, parents find themselves standing over the stovetop boiling water to place the bottle into

*Yup, you guessed it! Get your Kiinde bottles on my Resource Page. It's all there for you, Momma! (Page 219)

for warming. Whatever you do, avoid using the microwave to heat milk. It can get way too hot and does not heat evenly. Also, microwaves kill off many good nutrients.* Doesn't that defeat the purpose? You are breastfeeding and pumping, doing all this hard work to give your baby the best. Not to zap it away in an instant because of the *micro-waves.* Think about it.

*https://www.healthline.com/health/parenting/how-to-warm-breast-milk

Instead, warm the milk between your hands until the chill is gone. How simple! It only took him about two or three minutes to warm it. Honestly, babies do not need super-hot milk. And that's not how milk comes out of the breast either. My boy was hungry so he took it anyway it came to him. If you find your baby wants it a little warmer than this hand-warming method, you can certainly run it under a hot faucet of running water. Either way, you can heat milk in these bags much easier than any bottle system I ever found.

After the milk was warm, my husband unscrewed the cap, and placed a clean nipple on top of the milk bag. There was a frame to place the bottle into for holding, as to not squish the bag. The best part of this entire system, was that the milk bags did not allow any air in. This was monumental for my boy to have less gas, less burps, and hardly any hiccups ever. Not to say he did not burp after every feeding, he sure did. But there were very few times he had projectile vomit or major spit-up. Believe me, I have heard stories! I can count on one hand the amount of times I got baby barfed on. It wasn't incredibly often and this bottle system simulates the closest to breastfeeding than any other bottle out there.

Once my husband was done feeding, the frame popped off and so did the nipple. The frame was reusable, the nipple washable, and the milk bag was completely recyclable. These bags were one-time use only so he placed it right into our recycle bin. The only thing left to do was wash the milk nipple. It simplified our lives so much, I cannot even tell you! No washing "used" milk bottles, or worrying about crusty milk at the bottom and how to scrape it off. It was seamless, it was awesome, and worked extremely well for our lifestyle. I highly recommend these!

Our son slept 12 hours a night (8:30pm – 8:30am) since we moved him into his own room at 4 months old. It has been a dream for my husband and me. We still get a chuckle out of how lucky we are to have such a wonderful boy. I am not sure if I gave birth to a magic super baby, or if all this research has made the difference. I hope this helps you and your family too. Sweet dreams!

15

HUNGRY MOMMA FOOD PREP

While I was pregnant, I did a ton of reading, looking up things I had questions about, and reading Mommy Blogs. One bright idea I took to heart was cooking food ahead of time. Specifically prepping two weeks' worth of dinners. I remember when my sister gave birth for the first time, she hired a home chef to make meals for her. We liked this idea so much, we decided to do it ourselves and it was a HUGE blessing!

Buy small, aluminum, disposable loaf pans and gather some of your favorite recipes that freeze easily.

The goal is to have a frozen pack of a complete meal, so when it is time to eat, you toss it in the oven and dinner is served! No cooking, no prep, just heating it up to enjoy. I don't recommend using the microwave, though. Microwaves have the tendency to zap away all the good nutrients you are trying to feed your body.*

*https://www.medicaldaily.com/microwaves-are-bad-you-5-reasons-why-microwave-oven-cooking-harming-your-health-250145

You want every vitamin and mineral to count for your recovery and your baby's best health. We created healthy versions of lasagna, mac and cheese, chicken casserole, chili, enchiladas, just to name a few. The nice thing about make-ahead meals, if you freeze them right, they will last a year. We didn't try to cook these all on the same day, we did a little here and there. I was due in September and we started cooking in July. We knew they would be fresh and would also last.

We aimed to make about two meals per week to have in our freezer. We prepped as we cooked our normal dinners. For instance, as my husband was making his famous lasagna, he was also prepping four dinners in those disposable tins. He would do all the regular prep- layer in the noodles, meat, and sauce. He did everything except cook it. Once it was in the tin, he wrapped it in aluminum foil, covered it in plastic wrap, and foiled it again to be freezer-ready. This was dinner for two nights! One for him, one for me! With a little thought and planning, we were able to prep meals for two weeks! It was the BEST because after a full day of baby care, nursing, feeding and napping, the LAST thing I wanted to do was cook or clean dishes!

Believe me, if you have the ability to prep dinners, it is a lifesaver! If you have an in-law or grandma or someone who can cook for you, then you are more blessed than we were!

Some women have a very hard time losing their pregnancy weight once the baby is born. I was extremely fortunate to have my weight come off rather quickly. I gained twenty pounds during my pregnancy and every single pound came off in about two months. My theory is: pay attention to *what* you eat. Make sure you are getting good quality food, filled with highest quality nutrients. Drink a TON of water, as this will help with your recovery and keep your breastmilk flowing. Every day I drank a large water bottle filled halfway with coconut water and the other half with high quality alkaline water. Hydration helps flush out toxins and encourages weight loss anyway, baby weight or regular weight.

As women, we are so prone to hopping on the next available diet. Please do not do this! There is no need to diet during this time or eat a salad every night for dinner. Sure, salad is great! But you need substance. If you are nursing, you will need to eat like a truck driver. Not to say go out and eat fast food, chocolates, ice cream and what not. Just don't try to severely restrict what you're eating at this point. Even though you are no longer preggers, you are still eating for two. Just in a different way. Nature takes care of us and our bodies know what to do. As you continue to nurse your baby, the weight will come off eventually. If you decided not to nurse, it may take a little bit longer. Try not to be too hard on yourself here. We all have different paths and just know you will get there eventually. Be patient and feel the blessing of holding your baby in your arms.

Becoming a milk factory takes some getting used to. The more nutrient dense your meals are, the more nutritious your milk will be. My husband's lasagna contained organic red tomato sauce, all natural cheeses, grass fed organic ground beef, and whole wheat lasagna noodles. No skimping here, he went all out! And after breastfeeding all day, it felt good to eat a big dinner to replenish, just in time for the second half of my twenty four hours which consisted of the night time feedings.

Night time feedings! This reminds me, to remind you: pre-pack all your snacks. Every time I breastfed I felt ravenous right after, as though I could eat a 24-ounce porterhouse steak! I cannot express how important it is to replenish immediately after a feeding. *As tired as you may be, do not fall asleep without eating!* I would pack my little cooler with my blue ice packs, right before bed, or sometimes my honey would pack it for me (bonus points for all those partners out there!). I bought a big case of coconut water cartons and a big case of granola bars. Each night we packed 2 coconut waters, a LARGE jug of water (I would refill my reusable glass water bottles with high quality, filtered alkaline drinking water from our filtration system), 2 granola bars, a sliced apple, a small container of peanut butter, two tangerines, some small bags of nuts or trail mix, and maybe a banana. It sounds like a lot, but I would eat it ALL most nights!

The other key components I packed each night, were all my "nibs and dibs" for nursing (the nickname my husband and I gave them, instead of naming each item every time): nursing cups, nipple shields, milk collection vile, milk bags for freezing, and the sterile container that kept them all together. The first few nights, I didn't bring them upstairs with me and it was rough, to say the least. Especially when my baby cried. I had to run around looking for things like a crazy person. I had to wake my husband to help me find stuff until we figured out the whole routine. After a week, I hopped online and bought a second set of "nibs and dibs" to keep upstairs and left the originals for downstairs. It was so much simpler!

In the beginning, I had feedings every two to three hours. This was very tough for me as a new mom. Sleep deprivation was a difficult thing to navigate, but it was part of being a mother to a newborn. You have to find a way to sleep as best you can, whenever you can. I was so thankful to be in the state of California at the time of his birth. My husband got six weeks off for paternity leave! This was such a blessing. He could help with the baby during the day while I napped. After I fed the baby at night, Dada would swaddle him and rock him back to sleep. For the first six weeks we were a solid team.

As my baby boy became a better sleeper, he dropped down to two nighttime feedings. One at midnight, and one at 4:00 am. Hubby's start day back to work was quickly approaching and I wanted him to be rested. Once the nighttime feedings were reduced, I would be the one to get up and feed because I wanted my husband to get good rest so he could focus on work the next day. I would be in charge of diaper changes, pacifiers falling out, and anything the little guy needed throughout the night. I had the option to nap during the day, but my husband did not. There was no sense in us both being tired messes. I was willing to sign up for the task. Of course, he would be there if I needed help, but I wanted him to rest as best as he could.

What made the entire nighttime feeding process easier for me was having close proximity to everything I needed. The baby was right at the foot of my bed in the bassinet and my snack pack next to my rocking chair, which was in the corner of our master bedroom. All I had to do was walk six steps to get to all of it. Another key thing I kept in this area was a tablet to stream my favorite shows so I could stay awake. I heard stories about moms falling asleep while breastfeeding after being so sleep deprived, dropping the baby, and one or both of them getting injured. I took every precaution to avoid this and kept myself awake. My tablet allowed me to do that, and thankfully, my husband sleeps like a rock so it didn't bother him at all. It also kept my retinas stimulated so there was *no way* I was falling asleep during this important time to focus on the baby. The added bonus was a little light so I could see what the heck I was doing, without having to turn on the overhead bedroom light.

All these things in place made me feel in control of my environment and helped me to breastfeed like a boss! I felt like, sleep or no sleep, I've got this. By writing this book, my goal is right here in a nutshell: giving you Mommas the tools **to** succeed. If you have everything at your fingertips, you feel powerful, like this Momma thing is all yours! Think of it as having a desk job. You would not sit down to work without: a computer, pens, paper, or highlighters. You would also need the stapler, tape, paper clips, and a telephone. Oh yeah, let's not forget the desk and ergonomically correct chair. These are all equipment for the job. So get your equipment ready for the baby nursing job too!

Another must have: the Boppy!* I actually registered for this item and ended up getting three of them! At first I thought, what am I going to do with three of these things? Guess what, I used all of them. One in my master bedroom for nighttime feedings, one downstairs on the couch for day time feedings, and the third in the car for running errands. I am not saying to go out and buy three, but if you are blessed with more than one, consider yourself lucky. It was much better than trying to do a nighttime feed and realizing I had to go all the way downstairs to get the one and only Boppy. That would have been miserable! Be prepared and things will run smoothly.

*By the slim chance you have not checked out my Resource Page, it's on page 219. LOL!

16

IN THE BEGINNING, DELIVER EVERYTHING

I wanted time to settle in, get to know my baby, and figure out our routine. I did not want to leave the house for two weeks, so we asked our family and friends to come visit us. It was tough for me to move around anyway, and feeding every 2-3 hours was quite cumbersome. Two weeks was a reasonable amount of time *for me* to get a handle on this baby thing. The thought of trying to shower, getting dressed, and jumping in the car to go somewhere, then arriving at the destination, it would be time to feed already. No thanks. I wanted to rest and settle in for a little while and find my rhythm. There is nothing wrong with taking this time for yourself and your baby to get to know each other. Take as long as you need. It could even be a month or more. If you had a C-Section, or a more complicated birth, you may need even more time to heal. There is no set time frame for this. Do what feels right for you and your family. Besides, the hospital staff encourages new parents to wait a week to give the baby a bath. I did not want to take him somewhere, get him all "germy," and then not be able to bathe him right after. But that's just me.

Since our meals for dinners were in our freezer already, we needed breakfasts, lunches, and lots of snacks! We opted for grocery delivery. This was THE BEST! Compile a list of easy breakfast and lunch foods that don't require you to fire up the stove and dirty a bunch of pots and pans. Like protein shakes or cereal and milk in the morning, sandwiches for lunch, canned soups with crackers, fruit, sliced cheese, etc. Cut up fruit and vegetables to snack on. Apples with peanut butter was one of my favorites. I did a lot of meals in my slow cooker since it would end up being only one pot to wash. Things like slow cooker chili, a whole chicken, ribs, hearty soups, and stews. Try to think of foods that have high fiber, vegetables, good protein, and most of all substance! You need energy as you make milk, heal your undercarriage, get your organs back in place, and hips and bones move back to where they were in the first place. Basically, you are rebuilding your entire body, including your skin bouncing back from being stretched to the size of a basketball. Eat, woman! You need the fuel at this crucial time. Anyway, my point is, what you eat matters. What you feed your growing baby while they are inside of you, really matters. And what you eat while breastfeeding matters most!

DIAPER DELIVERY

What an amazing concept! This took away the fear of ever running out of diapers. And, yes, it was a genuine fear of mine, and I've honestly had nightmares about it. But how was I to choose whether I wanted disposable diapers or cloth diapers? Both can be delivered. But which was better for my baby? To each their own, but here is my take.

My husband and I went back and forth as to whether or not we wanted cloth diapers or disposable. I watched my sister and her husband diaper three kids using this awesome cloth diaper delivery service. The service would pick up the dirty ones and deliver a fresh batch every week. It worked really well for them, as they would order extra diapers to take with them whenever they went on vacations. It was an excellent system for their family. My brother-in-law is very focused on recycling, conservation, and leaving a smaller carbon footprint. In fact, so much so, we call him "Captain Planet!" I have always admired this about him, as he encourages my sister and their kids to be more conscientious. You go, man! It was important to him and their family to do diapers in this way.

If I could get past the "ick" factor, I may have done it too. But what got me was when I babysat their first two kids while they went to an annual Christmas party. Their boy was three and their daughter was one. The boy was pretty much out of diapers, which was helpful, but he was sick. He had a big cough, congestion, fever and was very fussy. I tried to put a warm water bottle on his chest to soothe his congestion, but he wasn't having any of it. As I tried to calm him down, the little sister made a HUGE poop. It was a total blowout which ruined all her clothes and almost my living room carpet. Ugh!

I tried to psych myself up and said. "Okay, get in there and do this!" It was a big job and in retrospect, I wish I had rubber gloves for that one! I did the best I could to save this cloth diaper. It was so gross, I just put her soiled diaper in a bag with the messed up clothes. I had no idea you needed to go to the toilet to dump the solids first and wipe it out as best as possible. Whelp, my brother-in-law gave me a good example of this when he got home. I watched him take the diaper, dump it into the toilet and then dip it in and out in the toilet water, to kind of wash it out. Eew! Then he placed it in a waterproof bag and held it for a week until the next shipment of clean diapers came to their house. That was sick and I didn't want to do that! I didn't and still don't really want to touch toilet water, like ever!

So it became a hard pass for me: NO to cloth diapers. And my husband did not hesitate to hop on *my* bandwagon. More power to those who go that route, as it was hard enough for me to clean up pee, poo, and milk-barf and have my own leaky milk boobs. I did not want to dip poopy diapers in the toilet water and keep them in my house for a week. Sorry man! Not for me! The choice became clear: disposable all the way!

TAKING BABY PLACES

The very first vacation we took was a big one, in an RV across the country from California to New York. He was only six weeks old. My in-laws lived in New York, and we didn't feel comfortable flying with a newborn. And no one in my husband's family liked to fly on airplanes, period. So, we found another way: to drive! When most people hear about this type of trip, with a 6-week old baby in tow, they are flabbergasted. The reason I bring this up is because my husband and I decided early on, we would **not** be one of those couples to say, "Oh, don't come over, the baby is sleeping," or "No, we can't go out anymore, since we have a baby now." These phrases never made sense to me. Why must your world stop because you "have a baby?" Oh, no... no... no! I was not doing that. Our little bundle was going to learn how to fit into our life. Not the other way around. Hence, a trip across the country. An overnight visit to my sister's house. Dinners out or a picnic at the park. Even a walk around the neighborhood. Don't be afraid to do these things, Mommas. Yes, it took me about a week or two to get myself together after childbirth. And honestly, there is no time limit here, ladies. Take as long as you need! But once you feel you are ready, go for it!

I eventually came to love my trips to Target, a lunch out with a girlfriend, or even a quick coffee at Starbucks, and yes, all with my baby alongside me! Let your little one see some stuff, and do things with you. There is a reason we got these fancy car seats, strollers, fully packed diaper bags, and changing systems. Taking a baby out to see new things is like watching a movie for them. It stimulates their little eyes with all this new stuff to see, excites their ears with new sounds, and pretty much tires them out completely. You will come to love the end result, which is a long nap afterwards. Well, what if you have to breastfeed while you are out? Guess what, you will! That is why you have a nursing cover up. That is what park benches are for. Trust me, it will be okay and you will find a way. I have pulled my car over and done it in a parking lot, in my back seat, because I could not make it home in time. We are resilient mothers, we are resourceful, and we will figure it out! Don't let that stop you from trying. You will go mad if you stay home for the next two to three years. Your life goes on. Plus, you need socialization and so does your baby!

17

MAKING MY OWN BABY FOOD

At six months of age, is when most Mommas introduce solid foods. I introduced him to his first bite on his six month birthday to the day. I knew early on, I did not want to feed him jarred baby food from the store. Most are full of preservatives and chemicals. It also bothered me that the expiration dates were so far away. I was not comfortable giving him food that could last on a shelf for a year or more. Others might be made with organics, but they still have a preservative added, to keep applesauce from going brown, and extending the shelf life. And the organic brands can be **extremely** expensive. Enter: homemade baby food.

We got a Ninja brand blender which was the largest volume container we could find and also had multiple blades throughout its center stem. This was key, since I made big batches of baby food, which would yield 10 -12 jars each time. At first look, this task seemed daunting, but it was certainly much easier once I got into the swing of things. For me, as an over producer of breast milk, I was able to use my own milk as the base for any baby food concoction I came up with. However, if you simply cannot spare the extra breast milk or decided not to breastfeed, any milk of your choosing will do: cows, almond, oat, or cashew milk. Just always try for organic. My boy's very first bite of life was a mashed banana with breast milk. I made sure I got it on video. He made the cutest little face of disgust, then surprise, and followed by deliciousness. It was so easy to feed him solids because it was something new and sweet. He loved it!

Some other recipes that fared well were steamed peas, boiled apples (no skins), and baked sweet potatoes. Now, thanks to the internet, you can pretty much look up any recipe there is. But I kept it very basic. It is important to introduce your baby to a variety of foods, but only one food at a time. Not only are they figuring out new tastes, but textures too. Up until this point, your baby has only had one type of texture and one flavor: milk. Thankfully, babies don't complain in this department, since milk is their favorite thing in the world! The need to transition them to taste each new food *separately* is 100% necessary. They need a slow process to taste new foods. And just because they may not like a certain taste at this moment, does not mean they will hate it forever. Keep on trying and mixing it up. Eventually, they will get it!

The best way to prep the food before turning it into baby food, is to steam it or boil it. Do not use any oil or butter on these, as veggies and fruits have to be as bland as possible. Use a metal vegetable steamer with the holes in it, the one that looks like a flying saucer. That's the one I used most. It worked quickly to steam on the stovetop and it only needed about one inch of water. Remember this one key for baby food prep, please: **DO NOT USE THE MICROWAVE!** You want all the nutrients to be whole and intact. As stated before, the microwave zaps the nutrients right out of them. This is the opposite of what we want, so keep it real and keep the food whole.

If you feel like doing a deep dive, try to google this question, "Does the microwave kill nutrients in food?" You will see the first response is put out by the USDA.gov. If you jump to page 10 of google, you will start to get the full story. I have not used a microwave for about 13 years. Honestly, I don't even have one in my house. Of course, you are free to make your own decision, but I encourage you to dig deep and learn for the sake of your health and your baby's health. The information is there, you just have to be willing to uncover it.

Sweet potato is an easy veggie to start with, since it is very mash-able and steams easily. I always used organics to avoid any unwanted chemicals or pesticides in the food. Slice vegetables in order to fit them into the vegetable steamer. I would either cube it or slice it into circles. Use a pot with a lid big enough to hold the vegetable steamer, and keep it covered so the steam can stay trapped in there to do its job. All you need is about one or two inches of water. Once the water comes to a boil, set a timer for 5 minutes.

Check them, and if a fork goes into them easily, they are done! I liked to keep the skins on to give my baby all the nutrients possible. Most vitamins are in the skin and it will blend nicely in the machine. Let the sweet potatoes cool and then add them to the blender.

When making your own baby food, you will want to use a milk of your choice to act as the base. If you are breastfeeding and have a surplus to use, that would be the best choice of all. If you are not breastfeeding, you may mix formula with water to act as your base. But formula-based baby food would need to be consumed on the same day. It does not keep as well as milk-based baby food, which can last up to three days. You may choose any milk you see fit for your child. There are lots of good nut milks: almond, cashew, coconut, etc.., But if your baby has a nut allergy, steer clear of nut milks. Maybe go for cow's whole milk, but get organic if you can. That would be the best choice for your little bundle to avoid all the chemicals that can be found in conventional milk. *(See Chapter 18 for more info on this.)* Sometimes people want to use low fat or 2% because that is what they have in the house. Keep in mind, whole milk has full fat which is best for your baby's developing brain, hair, skin, and basically everything! But if your baby has tummy troubles, there is lactose intolerant milk too. Take a stroll down the milk aisle. You are bound to find a milk that is right for your baby. Remember, this is the first food of life (other than breast milk or formula, so it is important to be as chemical free as possible.)

Blend the sweet potatoes first on their own in the blender, and as it is blending slowly add your milk of choice. Our lid had a little cap I could open to pour liquids into while still keeping the cover on it. This was helpful, so as not to get baby food all over my kitchen ceiling! As you add more milk, you will soon get it to the consistency you want. Aim for it to be a little bit looser than the mashed potatoes you might have on your Thanksgiving table. You want it a little bit thick, but not watery. It most likely won't pour out if you try to pour it, but get a large spoon or thin spatula and you can scrape it out into the baby jars.

Jars! I put a blast on Facebook to any of my friends who may have any leftover baby food jars from feeding their own kids store bought baby food. Unfortunately, everyone I knew had kids that were out of the baby food stage, or were only just getting pregnant. No one I knew was at this exact point of babyhood with me, so I was forced to buy a dozen baby jars with lids. This was truly one of my best investments. I used and reused these jars over the course of the next year. It made it so easy to lay out 12 clean jars on the counter and fill them directly with the fresh food I just made. All the lids were there and I didn't have to search for mismatched plastic lids that get lost in that random abyss of a cabinet we all have in our kitchens. I did not want to struggle to make his food, so having all my tools in place was key. Also, I knew I wanted to use glass so the chemicals in plastics would not leach into my baby's food. Here I am working so hard to make the "best in the west" homemade baby food, all organic, with fresh ingredients. Why on earth would I want to destroy it with plastic chemicals? I wouldn't. Hence, glass baby jars are the best. Not only are they dishwasher safe, easy to fill, but can also reuse them later on once my baby completes this stage.

After I filled the jars and secured the lids on tight, I would strategically line them up in my fridge. Knowing I had twelve servings of food ready to go along with my breastfeeding, I felt very accomplished.

It was a wonderful, freeing feeling of being prepared. I have always planned ahead and organized to help me live my best life. I did not want to be a mom who woke up, not knowing what was on the menu for the day, and having nothing made. Then, standing in front of the refrigerator with the door wide open for fifteen minutes trying to figure it out with a crying baby. This scenario would not be good for my anxiety level, or me feeling good as a mom. Nor would it be good for my little baby, who just wants to eat, sleep and be a baby. Just know, with a newborn, you will be the most sleep deprived in your entire life! It took me a solid four months to come out of the fog and start to feel somewhat normal again. Anything you can do to help yourself in advance, will be the best thing for *your* sanity and peace of mind. And your baby! Be the best you can be for yourself and your new little bundle. They are counting on you!

Photo by Me

Having these jars ready to go made them easy to toss into a cooler lunch bag with the blue ice packs. If I knew my baby and I would be out most of the day, I would bring this pack along with me, making sure to keep it cold. Breastmilk can stay out of refrigeration for about 4 -6 hours. I was never gone longer than that, since my errands only consisted of a run to the store, or a coffee date with a girlfriend. It was so much easier to have the jars of food ready to grab for my day, than trying to sit there and make it every morning. I highly encourage big batch making to save yourself some time.

The point of this section is to break it all down for you and hopefully simplify the baby food making process. Yes, I was a stay-at-home mom and had more time on my hands than say, a working mom. To all those working Mommas, I applaud you! If making your own baby food sounds super annoying, then pass on it. I am not trying to say every mom *must* do this. I am just sharing what I did. Sure, there were times when I would grab a baby food pouch from the store, if my boy was fussy that day and did not eat what I prepared for him. One time I even left the lunch pack sitting on my kitchen counter and all that food and milk I prepped had spoiled. Life happens. Motherhood is a journey and a struggle sometimes. Things do not always flow smoothly. Every mother knows that! We all do the best we can, the best way we know how. It is not the end of the world if your baby eats jarred food. But keep reading and feel encouraged. I hope you try it if you want to.

If you are ready to make your own baby food, here are some things to try. When I was doing this, I would make a different batch every time until I made my way through this list. I wanted my baby to try everything. Starting them at a young age can widen their flavor profile so they will have an advanced palette in the future and be able to enjoy all types of cuisine.

RECIPES

Start with the easiest foods first. These two require NO COOKING, as you just need to wait for them to ripen. This made my baby food making days easy to plan. I could grocery shop days in advance and have avocadoes and bananas on my countertop. If grocery shopping wiped me out, I had time to recover. Surviving in this sleep deprived world of mommy hood, I would usually attempt one major task per day. Grocery shopping would be on one day. Baby food making would be on a different day. It felt good to know I had all the supplies ready when the time came.

AVOCADO BABY FOOD RECIPE

1 or 2 whole ripe organic avocadoes

½ cup - 1 cup milk of your choice

Slice avocado open and remove the pit.

Place the avocado "meat" into the blender. Discard the skins.

As you blend, slowly add milk until you achieve the desired consistency.

Scoop into baby jars, seal with lids, and refrigerate.

It will keep for three days.

BANANA BABY FOOD RECIPE

1 or 2 ripe organic bananas

½ cup - 1 cup milk of your choice

Peel banana and place in the blender.

As you blend, slowly add milk to achieve the desired consistency.

Scoop into baby jars, seal with lids, and refrigerate.

It will keep for three days.

These next two recipes require one extra step: steaming. It's really not much of a burden, since they only steam for five or ten minutes. Just be sure to add some time to cool them in the refrigerator before blending with milk.

It is important to peel the carrots so you don't give your baby the tough exterior. Carrots get softer and blend better when using the inside only. As a side note, you can also choose baby carrots if you want to skip the step of peeling. Since they are already peeled they can save you time if you are feeling overly exhausted. I know I used baby carrots often in order to make it easier on myself. But still, always reach for organic whenever possible.

CARROT BABY FOOD RECIPE

2 or 3 whole organic carrots (peeled)

½ cup - 1 cup milk of your choice

After peeling the carrots, slice them so they fit into the vegetable steamer and place in a pot on the stovetop.

Add one inch of water to the bottom of the pot and place the lid on top.

Steam for 10-15 minutes until they are soft when poked with a fork.

Place them in the fridge to cool for about 10 minutes.

Once cooled off, add carrots to the blender.

As you blend, slowly add milk to achieve the desired consistency.

Scoop into baby jars, seal with lids, and refrigerate.

It will keep for three days.

With this sweet potato recipe, skins on gives your baby added nutrients. Just be sure to wash them well, as you would all your vegetables and fruits before making them. I like to use an all-natural fruit and vegetable wash that has very simple ingredients I can pronounce. Clearly, you are not trying to add more chemicals here, so read labels on all your products.

SWEET POTATO BABY FOOD RECIPE

1 or 2 organic sweet potatoes

½ cup – 1 cup milk of your choice

Wash sweet potatoes, slice or cube them, and place in vegetable steamer SKINS ON! The skins will blend nicely and contain many good vitamins and nutrients for your growing baby.

Add to a pot on the stovetop for steaming.

Add one inch of water to the pot and steam with lid on, for about 8-10 minutes, or until the sweet potatoes are tender when poked with a fork.

Drain the water and place potatoes in the refrigerator to cool them off (about 10 minutes).

Once cooled, add them to the blender.

As you blend, slowly add milk until you achieve the desired consistency.

Transfer to baby jars with lids and refrigerate.

It will keep for 3 days.

I also made some yummy fruit recipes, which my baby loved! I tried to keep a healthy balance of fruits and vegetables. Once he got past the beginning stages of trying every type of food for the first time, I knew what he liked, which was everything! I could then alternate and have both a fruit batch and a vegetable batch on hand so I could mix it up! Taste your food too, Momma! You will see the fruit ones are much sweeter than the vegetable ones. But you want your baby eating all types of food, not just the sweet ones. Hopefully, he or she will be excited to try all of them. And getting your baby to eat vegetables this young will set them up big time for loving them as a toddler.

Notice in the fruit recipes there is no skin, and fruits get boiled instead of steamed. But, after boiling them, you can use some of the water, once cooled, to add to the baby food mixture in the blender. This gives some added nutrients that were lost during boiling. They will still take the same amount of time as the vegetable recipes to cook. The only added step is fruit gets peeled, since babies under twelve months cannot digest the skins yet. Please do not skip this step, or your baby will be up crying with gas and tummy troubles.

PEAR BABY FOOD RECIPE

3 or 4 organic pears (CORED & PEELED)*

½ cup – 1 cup milk of your choice

½ cup nutrient-rich water after boiling pears

*It is important to peel the pears since babies cannot digest fruit skins until after 12 months.

In a medium pot, place peeled and cored pears and cover with water.

Bring to a boil, and continue to boil for 5-7 minutes, or until tender when poked with a fork.

Once done, set some water aside to use in this recipe. This water is very rich in nutrients for the baby, and comes in handy if you are trying to extend your breast milk supply.

Drain the rest of the water and place pears in the refrigerator to cool.

About 5 minutes.

Once cooled, add them to the blender.

Blend, slowly add milk & saved water to achieve the desired consistency.

Scoop into baby jars, seal with lids, and refrigerate.

It will keep for three days.

APPLE BABY FOOD RECIPE

3 or 4 whole organic apples (CORED & PEELED)*

½ cup - 1 cup milk of your choice

½ cup nutrient water after boiling apples

*It is important to peel the apples since babies cannot digest fruit skins until after 12 months.

In a medium pot, place peeled and cored apples and cover with water. Bring to a boil, and continue to boil for 5-7 minutes, or until tender when poked with a fork.

Once done, set some water aside to use in this recipe. This water is very rich in nutrients for the baby, and comes in handy if you are trying to extend your breast milk supply.

Drain the rest of the water and place apples in the refrigerator to cool. About 5 minutes.

Once cooled, add them to the blender.

Blend, slowly add milk & saved water to achieve the desired consistency.

Scoop into baby jars, seal with lids, and refrigerate.

It will keep for three days.

PEACH BABY FOOD RECIPE

3 or 4 organic peaches (PITTED & PEELED)*

½ cup – 1 cup milk of your choice

½ cup nutrient-rich water after boiling peaches

*It is important to peel the peaches since babies cannot digest fruit skins until after 12 months.

In a medium pot, place pitted and peeled peaches and cover with water. Bring to a boil, and continue to boil for 5-7 minutes, or until tender when poked with a fork.

Once done, set some water aside to use in this recipe. This water is very rich in nutrients for the baby, and comes in handy if you are trying to extend your breast milk supply.

Drain the rest of the water and place peaches in the refrigerator to cool. About 5 minutes.

Once cooled, add them to the blender.

Blend slowly, add milk & saved water to achieve the desired consistency.

Scoop into baby jars, seal with lids, and refrigerate.

It will keep for three days.

No need to be nervous or hesitant about making your own baby food. It is much easier than you think, Mommas. You will feel such incredible "Mom Power" making it and knowing exactly what goes into your baby's belly. Having the strength to go against the norm and create food the old fashioned way. Before store bought jarred food, before food came from a conveyor belt, and getting back to basics. You can do it, so go for it!

18

THE END OF AN ERA

My little guy started getting his first teeth around three months, and by six months old he had a full set. I found great success with the frozen teething rings and rubbery toys for him to bite on. When your baby starts teething, everything is fair game to get chewed on. I especially loved the jewelry meant for teething babies (necklaces and bracelets.*) He was learning to eat solid foods and learning to use his teeth. I was so thankful my nipples had "toughened up" over the past

*Available on my Resource Page at the back on page 219

eight months during all these feedings. Even though he was well on his way to eating solids, I was still feeding him my breast milk three or four times a day. Plus, pumping at night to get that full bottle for my husband to feed him.

One afternoon, I was breastfeeding him, and out of the blue, he bit me. Hard! Yes, this is a thing and your reaction can curb the biting if you react quickly. Unfortunately, I did not know how to react in that moment. I immediately took him off and handed him to my husband. Thank goodness he was home! I had to catch my breath and figure out what just happened. For 8 months, I fed my little baby peacefully, sweetly, drinking in every moment with him as he drank in all the nutrients from me. It was a mutual understanding we both shared and it was lovely, until now. This scared me and I wasn't sure how to proceed. I stopped the feeding session and gathered myself. I pumped the other side and had my husband feed him the rest through a bottle.

I immediately called my sister and my mom to get their take on the situation. My sister breastfed her children up to 17 months, which was the goal I was shooting for if I could make it. I wanted my son to have the *biggest* advantage he could with the most nutrients from breast milk, a.k.a. "liquid gold." They both experienced biting and deemed it as something you have to "work through" as a mom. My sister told me to flick his cheek next time he does it, tell him "NO!" sternly, and stop the process, so he knows he will not get any more milk until he behaves. Mom reassured me that part of being a mother means you must make these hard decisions. Some women choose not to breastfeed for their own reasons. Other Mommas are able to breastfeed for up to two years, or as long as they see fit. The fact that I made it 8 months was more than some ever get. It would be okay if I chose to stop breastfeeding, but also try to push through, as it would be best for the baby. I was extremely torn over this.

I later hopped online to see what to do about this whole biting thing. One tip was to set the baby down, walk away, and come back once you are out of pain and can to resume feeding. But babies have the natural urge to bite, especially after six months once they have eaten solid food. And, as teeth are coming in, they always want to gnaw and teethe on something to help their gums feel better. Apparently, my nipples were being used for this! I was in too much pain. Another technique I found online was to switch sides immediately after getting bit, to keep the milk going while the bitten breast rests. Keep switching back and forth! Are you kidding me? This made no sense to me because then you would have no "good nipple" as they would both become chew toys. Ouch!

Well, the next few feeding sessions were okay, no biting. But a few days later it happened again. A big chomp and this bite was harder than the last. It brought me to tears. I took some of the advice and immediately took him off, flicked his cheek and told him NO in a stern voice. It didn't really phase him. I waited a few minutes, before I tried to feed him again. I explained to him how things were going to be. I told him I could not take this biting thing. I have no problem stopping breastfeeding if this is how it is going to be. You are doing this to yourself little `man, and if it happens *one more time*, I am calling it quits. Three strikes and you are out! He listened as we finished the feeding session. Granted, he is only 8 months old, but I knew he could hear my tone of voice in that moment. I think he understood, but I wasn't quite sure.

A few days went by with no more biting, which gave me hope. Perhaps it was just a phase and the biting thing was over. NOPE! Sure enough, he bit me a third time, harder than ever before. I took him off my breast, and saw he had actually punctured my skin and drew blood! This was it. I did not even try any techniques, as I was seeing stars. Thankfully, my husband was home again to take over the feeding from a bottle. Why I am telling this awful story? Because I think it is important for mothers to hear every possibility that can happen to them, Yes, I heard about me biting my mom. But I didn't know the details. I guess this was my Karma payback for biting her. But still, I had to make a choice on what I was going to do.

I pumped and bottle fed him from this point forward, still struggling with the fact that this may or may not be the end of breastfeeding. I was so torn on what to do. About a week later, I had a meeting at the lactation club I belonged to. I highly recommend joining one to meet new mothers, get some education, and support for nursing. The club is called La Leche League and I have been going since he was born. They have chapters internationally, so check online for one near you. At first, I felt embarrassed to go to the meeting, since I had not breastfed him for about a week. We always sat in a circle and fed our babies while we chatted and listened to the moderator. She shared a story or a tidbit of information to help us along our breastfeeding journey. Moms can chime in if there is anything on their mind or an issue they are working through. Through tears, I shared about my son biting me while breastfeeding. It was a difficult thing because I felt like my son had turned on me. And I felt like a horrible mother for stopping breastfeeding and not working through it. I was seeking advice on how others faced this dilemma if there were any in my same situation.

The moderator gave me the best advice. As mothers, we are all on the same journey: Motherhood. It is like taking a hike up a long mountain trail. We start at the bottom when we give birth, and work our way up to the top. Reaching the summit is when your child turns 18 and you can release them into the world as an adult, knowing you did the best you could as their mom. Breastfeeding is just a small part of the journey. This is me stopping in a meadow to take a break, smell some flowers, and reflect on the journey.

Every mother's climb is their own. Every mother has a different path. Some of our paths will cross and others will go in opposite directions. Some mothers walk together for a while before they go off in another way. But we all reach the summit, one way or another. If I choose to let breastfeeding end in this meadow and continue on without it, let it be peaceful. I brought him through eight months of life with the "liquid gold." Some babies never have one drop. I should be proud. I have come this far.

Hearing this gave me great comfort. I understood I had done more than others. Still others had done more than me. But my path is my own. Their path is their own. Do not compare, do not compete. Focus on your baby and your journey together. After this meeting, I let breastfeeding stay in the meadow and continued on my journey without it. I could still pump to bottle feed him and use my milk in making his baby food. I realized this would work out the best for me, and he would still benefit from my milk. I switched him over to organic baby formula mixed with high quality, extra filtered alkaline water. My milk supply started to dwindle since the pumping was not as often as the feedings were with him. That was okay. I still got one more month of feeding him breast milk by pumping. And it took me about another two weeks to use up the supply in my freezer. All in all, he got breast milk up until he was 9 ½ months old. I should be very proud of this and I was. It was a blessing. He did not cry, it was not difficult to wean him off the breast. (I have heard stories!) He did not seem to miss it at all. My son became more interested in solid foods. And he seamlessly transitioned to the formula. Honestly, I don't even think he knew the difference, as he didn't miss a beat! I was proud of him and my decision.

I fed him formula up until his first birthday. After speaking to his pediatrician, he could come off the formula and switch over to regular milk. At the time, I could not find any organic cow's milk easily accessible. Through the years I have studied the farm practices of conventional farmers and non-organic milk compared to organic milk. I already knew I did not want to subject my new baby boy to the chemicals contained in conventionally farmed milk. Some USDA cows get injected with steroids and hormones to grow faster. They also eat grass which is often sprayed with pesticides and herbicides, which in turn, leaches into their milk. These chemicals are dangerous for a developing child to consume and can result in major health issues later on. Some have been linked to different types of cancers, neurological disorders, diabetes, and more diseases.* Our food system in America is seriously flawed. I could write a whole other book on this subject alone. I did not want to expose my perfect baby, who has only eaten organic food and my milk his whole life, to this nonsense. So I chose almond milk. It had the same amount of calcium as its cow milk counterpart, without the chemicals. And he loved it. All in all, the breastfeeding chapter was closed, and I became more than okay with it.

*https://beyondpesticides.org/dailynewsblog/2020/07 /from-udder-to-table-toxic-pesticides-found-in-conventional-milk-not-organic-milk/

19

NEW ADVENTURES
WITH MY BABY

Something very important to me was to get my baby
into the swimming pool as soon as possible. I have
seen videos of babies being thrown into the pool just
only one or two months old and they instinctively
know how to float and blow air out. This method may
work for some, but it was NOT for me. It terrified me
to see a little baby chucked into the deep end by one
parent while the other parent was underwater filming

with their camera. This was certainly not the type of swim lesson I wanted to do. But good for you, if you can stomach this. With my brand new baby, it was just too scary for me.

I swam competitively growing up since age 5 and all throughout high school. If I had any superpower to pass on to my child, swimming would be it! I wanted to get him into the pool as soon as possible, by following the footsteps of my mom. What she did for me worked and I wanted to continue the legacy. She got each of us, my sisters and me, into the pool by the time we were six months old. That was my goal as well. I signed up for the "Mommy and Me" swim class at our local YMCA. I got his little baby swim trunks, swim diapers, baby rash guard shirt, and hooded pool towel. It was overly adorable and I loved getting all set up. When I registered him he even got a baby membership card!

Walking into the YMCA made my heart race a little bit. The smell of chlorine hit me in the face like a brick as I walked through the lobby. Even though it was such a familiar smell and made me feel home again, I was so scared for what was to come with my little guy. He had no idea what was in store. Here I was taking my six-month old baby into a large pool of water. I knew I had to swallow the lump in my throat and just power through like my mom did before me. It was the best thing for him, even though it might have been a little tough for me in that moment. I held him in the water with me and I knew I was an excellent swimmer, but it was still terrifying.

Our first class was nerve-racking, but as the class went on, we both got more and more comfortable. His tiny swim trunks puffed up with air when I first put him in the water. His eyes grew gigantic like saucers when I brought the water up to his shoulders, like he was really loving it. He started splashing right away! That's when I knew, this would be a glorious adventure for us both. If you think bath time was cute, this was bath time on steroids! I poured water on his head, and watched his bangs stick to his baby forehead. He was the most adorable little swim bug I ever saw! I tried to maintain my composure when the instructor asked us to put the baby's face and mouth under the water so they could blow bubbles. This took some serious courage to do, and the instructor was very patient with all of us. But we did it! Eventually with this class, after weeks of swimming, he could stay under water for seven seconds! We worked up to it adding one second each week. I was so proud of him and proud of myself for being courageous together through this awesome adventure.

Part of being a mom is trying new things together, even though they may scare you a little (or a lot!) deep down inside. Nine times out of ten when I feel nervous about starting something new, like this swim class, his cuteness takes over so intensely that I forget all about any fears or doubts I ever had! Babies are magic that way. Little tiny wet toes wiggling and kicking in the water. Adorable prune-y little fingers and shiny wet cheeks. Oh and that smile! He loved it so much, I could tell he was going to take after me in this area. I was a water baby, always wanting to swim or be in the ocean and never wanting to come out. Already he loved it on the first day. That was my boy! So I encourage you, Mommas, to get out there and take your babies places, do new things. If swimming is not your thing choose something else that may work well for you and your baby. Maybe "Mommy and Me" tumbling class, music class, or story time at the library. There are so many ways to get your baby out and doing fun activities if you choose to. It may feel like you are going out of your comfort zone, but that is good for you and your baby. We all get scared and it is going to be okay!

GOING TO THE DOCTOR

Another example of new adventures was going to the doctor. His first appointment was rough because he didn't like being poked and prodded. In all honesty, who does? And naturally, whenever he needed a shot he lost his marbles, crying and screaming. This was extremely hard for me to watch as a mother because there was nothing I could do to help him. Until I realized, there was something! I had an idea and thought it might help so I searched far and wide for a little kid's toy doctor kit. I thought that maybe if we could pretend doctor stuff at home, he would get a little more comfortable when we had to go for real. As a new Momma, you will be going to the doctor A LOT in the beginning to get all those measurements, shots, and check-ups. Learning about how the doctor kit works is a visual way to explain to him what takes place in a safe environment at your own home. He took to it right away because it was a fun game we could play.

My kit contained a stethoscope, so I put it on and listened to his heart. Then I let him try it on me. Each step of the way, I explained which one of us was the doctor and what we were doing. Checking the heartbeat. I had a little fake shot to give him in his arm. Then he got a turn to give me a shot. There was a little thermometer to check the temperature in the ear. I checked his then he checked mine. This little exercise was very fruitful, and we would play every couple of days. Sure enough, next time he went to the doctor, he was very calm and knew what to expect with each instrument. I highly recommend this if your child becomes a handful at the docs. It worked great!

TURNING ONE YEAR OLD

We came upon his first birthday quick! It was unbelievable that one year ago I gave birth to this amazing little boy. My little monster, I called him. I went with a little monster party theme for his special day. I bought every monster decoration I could find: monster cups, plates, tablecloths, party favors, streamers, and more! I even ordered a monster smash cake from the local grocery store. When he ate this cake, it was his first sugar of life! After much discussion, my husband and I agreed we did not want to deny him his own birthday cake. And I had so much to plan, I was not up for the challenge of baking him a gluten free, sugar free, organic cake. UGH! That was too much to think about! Maybe next year. I felt so empowered knowing he made it an entire year without *any* sugar, which was huge for us. He didn't smash the cake like I wish he did, but he sure enjoyed it and made a mess of himself. Bright blue frosting stained his tongue for a little while. And as a heads up, it also makes for some interesting diaper changing later on. I never thought I'd see blue poo! Sure enough, he had a sugar crash and took a FAT NAP after his party. Success!

My boy, one year old! Everyone says time goes by so fast. Soaking in every moment helped me remember them once they are gone. I can take myself back to the times I rocked him to sleep in my rocking chair. Him resting his head upon my shoulder, and singing his favorite lullaby as he drifted off to sleep. All so precious. Drink it in, Mommas! Try to cement these moments into your memory so you can call upon them years from now. Tell yourself you can drink it in and you will. I did. Stay present and in the moment. Easier said than done, I know, but just know it CAN be done if you try for it. Take lots of pictures and videos, journal, talk to your precious baby so you know they recognize your voice, your memories, and your life together. It is a beautiful thing to share with each other. Memories last forever!

20

GETTING YOURSELF TOGETHER

As my book winds to a close, I want to take this last chapter to discuss a very important part of Mommy-hood. I think each and every one of us has struggled with, and will continue to struggle with until the end of time: self-appearance. I can only speak from *my* experience on how it has affected me. The first six weeks after childbirth, I did not wear a stitch of makeup! My wardrobe consisted of flowy palazzo pants, tank tops, and nursing bras. I still enjoyed a few choice maternity outfits, but nothing too fancy at all.

It was all about me being comfortable and finding my groove of feeding, changing and caring for this new little bundle. I am here to tell you, it's okay! Take as long as you need to get back to reality. After six weeks, we hit the road on our cross country RV trip from LA to NY. After a few days, I became very aware of how many pictures we were taking along the way. Pictures are forever, people! At first I would duck out of them and just capture my little dude and his Dada in the beautiful scenery. Then I started entering the frame, wearing sunglasses or a baseball cap (or both). I soon began to realize, this is not who I am. I can put in a little more effort here. I don't really want to be remembered in *this* way. Or not remembered at all, if I'm not even in the picture! I need some sort of proof that I was even on this trip, or one day, looking back, my son might say, "Mom, where were you?" Yes, although I was extremely sleep deprived, I still wanted to be in the pictures, and look like *myself* in them. When I show my son, years from now, I don't want to look like a ghoul with dark circles under my eyes. So, I figured out a simple Mom-tested, Mom-approved beauty routine. Much more simple than my regular routine, but still served its purpose.

I use very minimal makeup. To do my makeup in the morning, takes eight minutes. Yes, I have timed it: eye shadow, eye liner, mascara, and eyelash curler. My lip gloss is Chap-stick. A touch of blush and that is it! My hair routine (Mom bun) takes about 30 seconds. But how I feel after these 8 minutes and 30 seconds is like I did a 180 and I can go out into the world with my head held high. I can make eye contact with people and my baby can see me with eyes wide open, not eyes wide shut. A little bit of fixing yourself up can make you feel good on the inside. Also, I think it is important to do what you feel to make yourself pretty for YOU and your partner. There I said it. Although my man may never admit it, I know I feel like "what the cat dragged in" sometimes. He tells me I am beautiful no matter what and I love him for that. But I want to make *myself* feel better. So in a round-about sort of way, I am doing it for him, but I am doing it for myself more! Find a way to do small things to make YOU feel better. Taking care of a baby can be exhausting. Keeping a positive view of yourself can be a balancing act.

As women, who have just given birth, we are faced with challenges men will never have to face:

stretched out bellies and boobs, cellulite, dark circles under our eyes, swollen ankles, and the list goes on. We are the ones who have the milk, and have to get up at all hours to feed the baby. We are the ones, who can't have sex for six weeks because our vaginas have to recover from the war zone that went on down there. And we are the ones who have to keep our heads held high in society, buying groceries, getting a Starbucks, or picking up more diapers. And there will be a time you run into an old friend on that *one day* you just rolled out of bed and look like a scary Halloween monster. Yes, it has happened to me! It is not a good feeling. I want to encourage you to put yourself together, just a little, for the sake of what it does for your self-esteem. It is for you, my darlings. And it feels good.

There was a time I was able to put myself together, get a little dressed up with a nice sundress and some jewelry. I had just fed my baby and we were on our way to Target to pick up a few things. Walking in, I treated myself to a Starbucks near the front of the store. I was feeling good about my day, balancing motherhood, and going out somewhere. After I paid and sat down to wait for my drink, I rocked my baby in his stroller, as he slept peacefully. I saw another Mom at a different table with her newborn. She was wearing stretch pants, had a milk-stained T-shirt, no make-up, and her hair was as if she just rolled out of bed. Now, she wasn't doing anything wrong or not dressed improperly. I know she was doing the best she could in that moment, and trust me, I have even been in her shoes. I have left the house just like her some days. And it's OKAY! The point I want to get across is the way *SHE* looked at *ME*. I could see the sadness in her eyes and envy of her thinking, "How does she have it all together? She has a baby just like me. Why does she get to wear makeup, have a nice dress on, AND have a cute baby?" Truth is, whether you get dressed in the morning into a pair of sweatpants or a nice sundress, the choice is ultimately yours! It takes the same amount of time to get dressed into either one. Here she was judging me, (I could feel it) for being out, seemingly put together, as if I was doing something wrong.

Let us stop judging each other. The road goes both ways. I could be judging her, thinking, "Geez, how can you leave the house like that?" And she could be judging me, thinking, "Why do you care more about your looks than your own baby?" Actually, it is neither. As women, we can't win either way! If you dress up too much, people can accuse you of not caring for your child and putting too much time into getting ready. While the baby might fuss or cry, all the while you are taking attention away from him. Nope, my boy was asleep so he didn't even know the difference. And if you put in no effort, you are seen as a hot mess. Our challenge is to find that healthy balance of not being too high maintenance and not just rolling out of bed. As women, we need to stand up for each other, not tear one another down. If you see a mom who just rolled out of bed, congratulate her and tell her she is doing a good job. That is what I wish I had done that day at Target. And put her mind at ease that me looking like this is few and far between. And if you see a mom that has it all together, congratulate her as well. Tell her you like her dress, or her hair looks pretty. We don't say these kind words to one another enough and we all could spread a little more love!

But let me be clear about **not** falling into the unrealistic expectations forced upon us by society. Just pick up any magazine or turn on a "reality" TV show. You will see the expectation and subconsciously you may want to achieve these looks that are photo shopped, air brushed with spray on make-up, and look so fabulous with the Hollywood lighting and camera tricks. Remember these women spend hours in hair and make-up in order to look flawless for the cameras. Don't fall for the hype! It is fake, so fake.

Once, out of curiosity, I googled "how to contour" and I watched a makeup video on YouTube. Whoa! Once this girl got to her 18th product of highlighter, contrast, tiger stripes, or whatever you call it, I was out! I think it was a 48 minute video. Geez, I didn't even have time for this when I was single, so certainly not now with a baby! If that is your thing, more power to you. But for me, I need simple, fast and easy.

And, it is not healthy to try and try, and never reach this unattainable look which is being forced upon us as women. At the very least, this can damage the way you see yourself. If you feel less than, you won't be at your best for your family. And your children will pick up on this negative energy. You cannot fill your child with love and acceptance from an empty cup. Fill your cup first and feel good about yourself. Do things that lift you up to feel fresh, rested, pretty, and fabulous in your own way. Then you will be ready to give your all to your family.

Once a month, I do my own pedicure at night to treat myself, after I put my little guy down. Soak my feet and everything which feels good after a long day. And I love looking down at sparkly toes. I also try to do fresh nail polish on my fingers once a week. It makes me happy to see color, flowers, or glittery nails. Put some pep in your step for you to feel great!

Be strong, be bold, and be beautiful, in your own way. Celebrate the color of your eyes. Marvel in the strength of your arms and legs, lifting these babies we bear. Applaud yourself when you wear your baby to do laundry, carrying him, and a heavy laundry basket at the same time. We are Mom Warriors! We don't need a chef to cook for us. We got this! We don't need a makeup and hair team, we are beautiful. Flip that gorgeous hair you grew while pregnant. You built baby and that baby built you into a Mom. Let that sink in. You built a baby and that baby built a Mom.

Go forth! No matter what stage you are in motherhood, take this knowledge and put it to good use. It is my gift to you. Start nesting. Join your local birthing class. Print out my checklists for each room.

It is all here, all for you. Raise the best child you can dream of! Be natural. Eat excellent food. Be beautiful. Celebrate this journey and do not be afraid of any piece of it: childbirth, changing a diaper, baby barf, breastfeeding, your healing birth canal, or any of it. Go forward with confidence. You now have the tools. You have the innate "mother's instinct" and millions of women have birthed babies before us. Now you can fine tune it to make this journey even better. Be encouraged! Thank you for gobbling up my book. I hope it serves you well, as it has been my ultimate pleasure to lay it all down on paper FOR YOU! So raise your glass, whether it be a cup of coffee, a glass of OJ, a water bottle, or your child's sippy cup. Cheers to all of you! Now go out there and prep for this incredible bundle of so much joy, you will be proud to call, *"My Baby!"*

ACKNOWLEDGEMENTS

God: Thank you for giving me the strength to write my story. And for gifting us women, the ability to carry and birth another life. I am so blessed to have my rainbow baby superstar!

Peter Famiglietti: Thank you, my dear husband. What started as a "twinkle in your eye" became our beautiful baby boy. You gave me courage to keep on going when all hope seemed lost. Thank you for walking with me on this path and continuing to be by my side through it all. I love you and I am so grateful to share my life with you, my love!

My Son: You are my rainbow baby. You are four years old as this book goes to print. I have seen you grow from this teeny tiny "Baby R" to the sweet, kind little boy you are today. You bring so much joy and laughter into our household. Without you, I would have no story. Thank you for being my boy and making me a Momma. I am so happy you are mine!

My Mom: Oh, my beautiful Momma how I miss you so! Although you are in heaven, I know you are smiling down on me. Thank you for raising me, guiding me, and teaching me all that you know. I miss you every day, but still feel your presence. I promise to honor you by sharing all the things you did for us as kids, with my boy. Like Mickey Mouse pancakes, cookies for Christmas, and all the spooks for Halloween. You might be gone, but your memory will live on forever!

Jenifer and Daryl Landis: My sister and my brother-in-law. I got the honor of holding each of your children when they were only one day old. I had the privilege to watch you raise three beautiful babies.

Through diapers and milk spit up, you taught me more than you know. Thank you for going before me and teaching me skills I could only learn by babysitting or watching you guys do it first. After all, that's what family is for!

Dr. Julie Taylor, MD: How can I ever thank you? You figured me out during a time when other doctors could not. You helped me carry my boy to term and I am forever grateful. I can only hope my story impacts other women enough to never give up trying. You were my ray of sunshine in a very dark place, and I thank you.

Dr. Carrie McDermott Goldman: How wonderful you were as my editor. When you agreed to take on this project, I would not have wanted anyone else. Your feedback and honesty meant so much to me, as I know you made me a better writer and helped me tie it all together. Huge hugs and a big thank you!

Angela Sheffield You were instrumental in putting the finishing touches on my book. You were so gracious with your time and copious notes. From one writer to another, I appreciate your dedication to my project. Thank you!

Every Momma (and Dad) who picked up my book, I would not be a writer without readers! You made my dream come true. Thank you for reading and sharing the love. I can only hope my story can inspire a generation of prepared parents and healthy babies. Wishing you all the success with your new little bundle.

RESOURCES

Here is the Cocoa Butter I used.
Scan this QR Code to get yours!

"19 Must Haves Before Bringing Baby Home"
Videos of me demonstrating every product I
discussed throughout my book. Visit:
www.myrockerbeez.com/for-baby

Print my "Room by Room Checklists," go to:
www.myrockerbeez.com/lists
Use Password: **Nesting**

To watch my Breathing Video visit:
www.myrockerbeez.com/post/breathing
Products for Mommas
Babies need a lot of stuff, but so do we!
The corset I used, the breastfeeding gear, stylish
diaper bag, and so much more!
www.myrockerbeez.com/for-momma

If you would be so kind as to leave me a review of my book, it would be SO APPRECIATED!

And follow me on all my social media accounts and I will follow back. I am **My Rockerbeez** on every single platform.

Sign-up on my blog with your email so you don't miss any bonuses or freebies. I also do a weekly recipe for busy Mommas sent right to your inbox!

Enter your email at:

www.myrockerbeez.com

AND IF YOU WANT TO HEAR MORE FROM ME, SUBSCRIBE TO MY NEW PODCAST CALLED:

"A MOMMY AND A MIC"

FOUND WHEREVER YOU GET YOUR PODCASTS!